W9-AYZ-738

What People Say About Taekwondo Grand Master Jhoon Rhee

"I met Jhoon Rhee in 1966. He is a great volunteer and has done a lot for our country. He is so famous that he is a great face for our great ally Korea. I respect him. I am pleased to recognize you as the 721st Daily Point of Light."

— Former President, GEORGE H. W. BUSH

"No one is a more effective promoter of US and Soviet relations than Grand Master Jhoon Rhee. His article shows the guiding principle for harmony among nations and between USSR and the USA."

— Former Cultural Attache for the Soviet Embassy, ALEXANDER POTEMKIN

"Master Rhee taught me Accu-Punch; it is so fast, you can hardly see it."

— World Heavyweight Boxing Champion, MUHAMMAD ALI

"Grand Master Jhoon Rhee is the best gift from Korea to the United States."

— Former Secretary of Agriculture, MIKE ESPY

"Master Jhoon Rhee stands tall among all great people of the world I have met. If the best of friends are golden, you are platinum."

— Chairman and CEO of Parade Magazine, WALTER ANDERSON

"To Taekwondo Grand Master Jhoon Rhee, whose constant love, loyalty and knowledge inspire me to greater accomplishments. I respectfully bow to you, sir. I learned a deeper sense of joy for life from you."

— World Renowned Speaker, TONY ROBBINS

"Master Jhoon Rhee is the best gift from Korea to the United States."

— Former US Secretary of Labor, ELAINE CHAO

"Learning Martial Arts from Grand Master Jhoon Rhee and receiving my black belt gave me the foundation to become a world class dancer. Grand Master Jhoon Rhee is an inspiration for all mankind and a true spiritual leader. He is a beacon of light."

— World Renowned Ballet Dancer RASTA THOMAS

"You are the best Taekwondo man I know; so you can do a Taekwondo movie."

— BRUCE LEE

"I might say Master Jhoon Rhee has become a national treasure."

— Chairman, US Armed Forces Committee US REP. IKE SKELTON

"Master Rhee is the greatest American I know. He is indeed changing the world."

— Former Speaker-elect, BOB LIVINGSTON

"Master Rhee defies the assumed rush of the years. He is an ageless patriot, whose brand of unbreakable loyalty is seldom seen."

— Former CEO, Motion Picture Association of America, JACK VALENTI

Published by TBL Publishing, Inc.
1450 Emerson Avenue, Suite G-03, McLean, VA 22101
First published 2010, TBL Publishing, Inc.
Copyright © 2011 TBL Publishing, Inc.

TBL Publishing, Inc. ISBN 978-0-9817838-3-3

Printed in South Korea

Hope of Healing the World

TRUTOPIA
The Taekwondo Philosophy

By
Grand Master
Jhoon Rhee

"When I am Truthful my heart is beautiful;
When my heart is Beautiful, people love me;
When people Love me, I am Happy."

Jhoon Rhee

Former Congressman Toby Roth and Grand Master Jhoon Rhee discussing strategies to help reduce American health care costs.

We are planning to develop a home-study black belt course program to motivate those who do not have the time to join local martial arts schools.

21 Miraculous Achievements by Grand Master Jhoon Rhee

Presented By
United States Congressman
Toby Roth

Lighting the World with Mutual Respect

Former President Ronald Reagan.

THE WHITE HOUSE
WASHINGTON

June 20, 1986

It gives me great pleasure to salute Congressmen Toby Roth, Bob Livingston, Bill Chappell, and the Honorable Richard Ichord as you are awarded the rank of Black Belt in Tae Kwon Do. Congratulations!

Tae Kwon Do promotes strength, coordination, fitness, and self-discipline. You've all worked long and hard for this well-deserved recognition. You have my congratulations and my warmest good wishes. God bless you.

Ronald Reagan

Former President George H. W. Bush during a visit on March 29, 2010.

GEORGE BUSH

August 18, 2010
for
September 30, 2010

Barbara and I send greetings to Master Jhoon Rhee as his friends and admirers gather in the Cannon Caucus Room to celebrate his 80th birthday and to honor his forty-five years of volunteer service to Members of Congress.

Jhoon Rhee is universally recognized as one of the world's greatest masters of Taekwondo. What might be not so well known about him, however, is that he has worked tirelessly to promote peace and harmony among nations, and for decades he has given unselfishly of his talent and his time to the youth of our Nation. Grand Master Jhoon Rhee is a true "Point of Light," and we Bushes are proud to call him friend.

Happy Birthday and all the best to you, my friend, Jhoon Rhee, for success with your new work, TRUTOPIA.

Sincerely,

G Bush

Table of Contents

Foreword

by Former United States Congressman Bob Livingston

Grand Master Jhoon Rhee is the greatest American I know. Of the many sorts of people in the world, few are of such indomitable spirit that they overcome the toughest of obstacles; he still maintains a sunny and optimistic conviction that people have it within their personal control to change the world eternally for the better. Despite his many years of survival of hardship against great odds, Grand Master Jhoon Rhee is one such person.

Born in Korea over 80 years ago, Jhoon Rhee was a young teenager when his country was ravaged by World War II and the Korean War. His very existence is a testimony to the phenomenal irrepressibility of human spirit under incredibly oppressive conditions. Yet he not only survived but prospered in his later life because of the loving friendship of a few wonderful American soldiers. He has never forgotten the appreciation he has for them and for the country they served.

Grand Master Rhee's first trip to America was on June 1, 1956, for a short military training program soon after the Korean War. He returned as a freshman at Southwest Texas State Teachers' College in San Marcos, Texas with $46 in his pocket in 1957. The English language was his biggest challenge. It took him a half hour to read a single page of a college text book during his freshman year. Through perseverance and discipline, Grand Master Rhee has become known as one of the most prominent public speakers in the world today. Indeed, the life of Grand Master Jhoon Rhee is a remarkable American success story.

I first met Jhoon Rhee in Washington, DC, over 25 years ago. I represented southeast Louisiana in the US Congress, and Master Rhee was rapidly becoming known as the Taekwondo instructor who was running ads in the DC area for his studios. "Nobody bothers me!" his three-year-old daughter Meme and four-year-old son Chun proclaimed as she knocked down opponents and broke boards for the TV camera.

Master Rhee has been volunteering his expertise as a physical fitness guru and instructor for various members of the House and Senate for several years. While I had never been athletic as a child, I had always been curious about martial arts, and it wasn't long before Master Rhee had me signed up for his class, which meant that I was booked at 7:00 a.m. virtually every Tuesday, Wednesday, and Thursday morning for several years.

One of my proudest memories was when I finally emerged with a Black Belt in Taekwondo with only a couple of modestly broken toes to show as war wounds along the way. It has been a long time since my last lesson, but I'm pleased to say that my friendship with Master Rhee has survived to this day.

Master Rhee is a marvel. At 5'6", he is a masterpiece of fitness and integrity. He would pride himself on being able to do 10 sets of 100 push ups throughout every day, a feat he would continue well into his 70s.

But he is also a musician. He choreographed all his workout routines to classical music, including Beethoven and Strauss. When his brother, a successful sports shop entrepreneur in New York City, mastered the harmonica and played more than one instrument at the same time, Grand Master Rhee the competitor practiced his own routine and performed at concerts with flawless exhibitions of harmonic dexterity, playing classical pieces with several harmonicas at the same time.

He is a consummate diplomat and has unabashedly devoted himself to the cause of promoting American democracy to the world, quoting our forefathers in greater content and with far better fluency than I have heard from most, if not all, American politicians. He has gone to every corner of the earth to proclaim his beliefs that freedom from tyranny is imperative for the development of the human spirit. He did so in the old Soviet Union before it collapsed and he has since gone to Russia and many of the emerging independent countries with the same message. He has traveled throughout Asia with his message of hope and optimism, and he successfully uses the message of physical fitness and his mastery of Taekwondo to gain entry into the most resistant of regimes to promote his cause. Moreover, his audiences love him and invite him back.

Grand Master Rhee believes he can change the world by inculcating youngsters with the physical and mental discipline to refrain from intoxicants of any kind, to work and study hard and to become productive contributors to the world around them through a wholesome commitment to decency. As a visionary with the energy to work toward his goals with as much vigor in his late 70s as he did when in his 30s; he is one truly remarkable human being. He is indeed "changing the world."

I, Jhoon Rhee, wrote an essay, "My Vision for the Third Millennium," in January 1998, proclaiming a happy global human society in the 21st Century. After sharing the essay with a dozen members of the US Congress during one of our Taekwondo classes, Rep. Bob Livingston wanted to introduce the essay into the US Congressional Record. I was very happy and honored. Rep. Bob Livingston introduced the essay on March 25, 1998 as shown below:

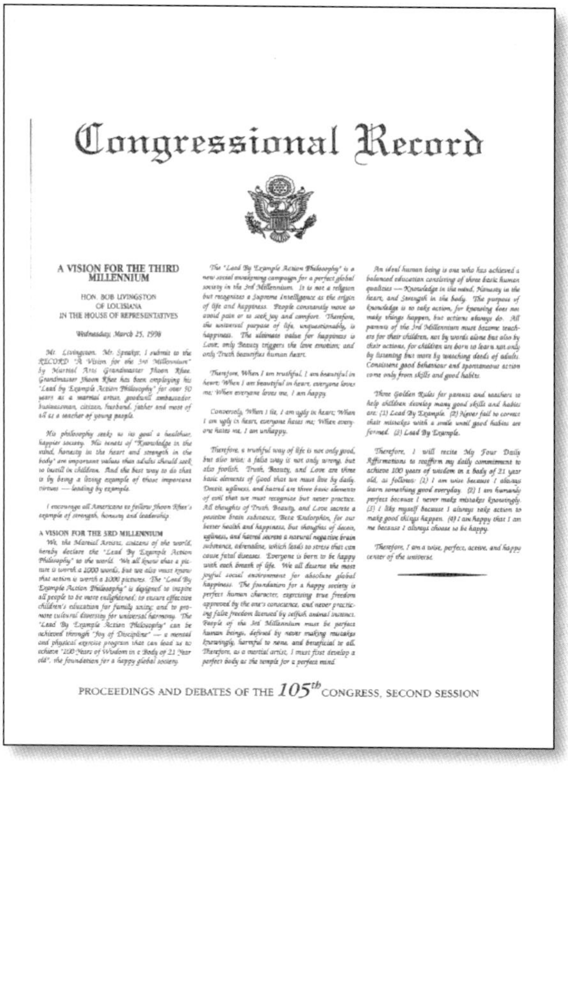

Congressional Record

A VISION FOR THE THIRD MILLENNIUM

HON. BOB LIVINGSTON
OF LOUISIANA
IN THE HOUSE OF REPRESENTATIVES

Wednesday, March 25, 1998

PROCEEDINGS AND DEBATES OF THE 105th CONGRESS, SECOND SESSION

Here is the text of the Congressional Record.

MY VISION FOR THE THIRD MILLENNIUM

HON. BOB LIVINGSTON of LOUISIANA
IN THE HOUSE OF REPRESENTATIVES

Wednesday, March 25, 1998

Mr. Livingston, Mr. Speaker, I submit to the RECORD "My Vision for the Third Millennium" by Martial Arts Grand Master Jhoon Rhee. Grand Master Jhoon Rhee has been employing his "Lead by Example Action Philosophy" for over 50 years as a martial artist, goodwill ambassador, businessman, citizen, husband, father, and most of all, as a teacher of young people.

His philosophy seeks as its goal a healthier, happier society. His tenets of strength in the body, honesty in the heart, and knowledge in the mind are important human qualities that adults should seek to instill in children. And the best way to do that is by being a living example of those important virtues—leading by example.

I encourage all Americans to follow Jhoon Rhee's example of strength, honesty and leadership.

My Vision for the Third Millennium

We, the Martial Artists, citizens of the world, hereby declare the "Lead by Example Action Philosophy" to the world. We all know that a picture is worth a 1000 words, but we also must know that an action is worth a 1000 pictures. The "Lead by Example Action Philosophy" is designed to inspire all people to be more enlightened; to ensure effective children's education for family unity; and to promote cultural diversity for universal harmony. The "Lead by Example Action Philosophy" can be achieved through "Joy of Discipline"—a mental and physical exercise program that can lead us to achieve "100 Years of Wisdom in a Body of 21 Years Young," the foundation for a happy global society.

The "Lead by Example Action Philosophy" is a new social awakening campaign for a perfect global society in the Third Millennium. It is not a religion, but recognizes a Supreme Intelligence as the origin of life and happiness. People constantly move to avoid pain or to seek joy and comfort. Therefore, the universal purpose of life, unquestionably, is happiness. The ultimate value for happiness is Love; only Beauty triggers the love emotion; and only Truth beautifies the human heart.

Therefore, when I am truthful, my heart is beautiful; when my heart is beautiful, people love me; when people love me, I am happy.

Conversely, when I deceive, my heart is ugly; when my heart is ugly, people hate me; when people hate me, I am unhappy.

Therefore, a truthful way of life is not only good, but also wise; deceiving is not only wrong, but also foolish. Truth, Beauty, and Love are the three basic elements of Good that we must live by daily. Deceit, Ugliness, and Hatred are three basic elements of Evil that we must recognize but never practice. All thoughts of Truth, Beauty, and Love secrete a positive brain substance, Beta Endorphin, for better health and happiness, but thoughts of Deceit, Ugliness, and Hatred secrete adrenaline, which leads to stress that can cause fatal diseases.

Everyone is born to be happy with each breath of life. We all deserve the most joyful social environment for absolute global happiness. The foundation for a happy society is perfect human character, exercising true freedom approved by one's conscience, and never practicing false freedom licensed by selfish animal instinct. People of the Third Millennium must be perfect human beings, defined by never making mistakes knowingly, harmful to none, and beneficial to all. Therefore, as a martial artist, I must first develop a perfect body as the temple for a perfect mind.

An ideal human being is one who has achieved an education consisting of three basic human qualities— Strength, Honesty, and Knowledge. The purpose of knowledge is to take action, for knowing does not make things happen, but actions always do. All parents of the Third Millennium must become teachers for their children, not by words alone but also by their actions, for children are born to learn not only by listening but more by watching deeds of adults. Consistent good behavior and spontaneous action come only by skills and good habits.

Three Golden Rules for parents and teachers to help children develop many good skills and habits are: (1) Lead by Example. (2) Never fail to correct their mistakes with a smile until good habits are formed. (3) Lead by Example continually.

Therefore, I recite My Four Daily Affirmations to reaffirm my daily commitment to achieve 100 years of wisdom in a body 21 years young, as follows:

1. I like myself because I always take action to make good things happen.
2. I am humanly perfect because I never make a mistake knowingly.
3. I am wise because I always learn something good everyday.
4. I am happy that I am me because I always choose to be happy.

"Therefore, I am one of the wise, humanly perfect, active, and happy centers of the universe." *Jhoon Rhee*

Jhoon Rhee, My Friend and Grand Master

By Former United States Congressman Toby Roth

Grand Master Jhoon Rhee is trying to create something everyone in the world has been aspiring to throughout history. I first thought he was out of his mind. The more I listened to him, the more I was puzzled and challenged by his logical explanations. But even so, he is talking about an ideal world in which everybody can be happy. Naturally, my initial reaction was, "Nonsense," and of course, I did not tell him this. He is one of my best friends as well as my Taekwondo Grand Master, a man whom I have known for the past 30 years.

Because I am one of his tens of thousands of Black Belt students, I felt motivated to write this biography. I thought I knew Grand Master Rhee well, I really did not, until I researched more closely his many hidden achievements; his "miraculous achievements." So now I want to share with you the incredible life Grand Master Rhee has been living for these last 80 years, beginning in the depths of the global Great Depression, born very humbly in one of the poorest countries in that desperately troubled world of 1932.

I urge readers to witness for themselves a few of Grand Master Rhee's miraculous achievements by watching the DVD included with this book.

I also want to introduce you to Grand Master Rhee's world-changing philosophy, TRUTOPIA. The Taekwondo philosophy of TRUTOPIA should have been written millennia ago to avoid all the hardships mankind has gone through since the beginning of human history.

But now at last, thanks to Grand Master Jhoon Rhee, we possess a series of logical but simple answers to millions of the complex problems piling up in our time. Grand Master Rhee has concluded that, fortunately, there is only one cause for all these millions of problems. I will let the Grand Master himself share what that one cause is with you.

Grand Master Rhee is one of the most patriotic Americans I know. I have never met anyone who promotes the American Freedom System more than he does. When I watch his video showing the Martial Arts Ballet he choreographed to the American National Anthem, being performed by people in eight different countries, I almost can't believe my eyes. I don't know how he persuaded so many foreign groups to learn a Martial Ballet choreographed to the American National Anthem. It's hard enough just trying to teach foreigners how to sing the National Anthem!

I have known Grand Master Rhee for over three decades, and I have never seen him emotionally down; he always carries a positive attitude through life. Being an American inspires the Grand Master. I once asked him: "What makes you think America is so great?" His answer was very simple and direct. "Because of the divinely-inspired Founding Fathers' mission statement for America created at the beginning of her history. To this day America still takes action according to that original mission statement." I will let Grand Master Rhee explain later what the mission statement of America was.

For now let me finish by pointing out that Grand Master Jhoon Rhee is the ideal person to blow America's horn because he looks like a foreigner. His views about the United States sound more objective to global audiences than would those of an average-looking American. And what Grand Master Rhee tells his worldwide audiences, is America was created, not only for the American people, but also for everybody on this planet.

Congressman Toby Roth breaks two boards during his black belt promotional test on June 24, 1986 in the US Senate Russell Building.

Introducing 21 Miraculous Achievements

Grand Master Rhee is talking about creating an ideal world. He is trying to share with you the truth about the original intent of the Creator, prior to creating the first man and first woman. The Creator intended to create, not some imaginary utopia, but a real utopian society, where everyone is healthy, wealthy, and happy—the Universe of Truth, Beauty, and Love (TBL) for the Happiness of every one of His children.

Grand Master Rhee realizes that no other thought can seem more insane than what he is promising to the world today. However, he obviously feels compelled to do so. He believes the true utopia is at hand. In order to realize such a task, first, one must have an idea, and second, one must have a plan of action. How is he going to realize this gigantic vision?

Here is how:

Grand Master Rhee's plan of action is to follow the universal creative principles, starting from simple to complicated, from small to large, from one model person to billions. We must start with one model person, then go on to one model school, then to one model city, to one model nation, and finally one happy global society. He calls this society (True + utopia = TRUTOPIA,) where everyone is healthy, wealthy, and happy.

Grand Master Rhee realizes that the first model person has to earn absolute trust, first from his or her spouse, who knows everything about that person better than anyone else. Then from that person's family members, all friends, and everyone who meets or hears of that person, and eventually everyone in the world.

The only way to develop absolute trust is to live nothing but Truth, Beauty, and Love (TBL), to treat others as you wish to be treated and to give more than you receive. The first person has to become a role model for others. There is only one cause for millions of social problems. The cause is the distrust created by selfish deceivers. What other cause is there? I cannot think of anything else. Therefore, all leaders of the world must concentrate on children's character education at early ages, starting in kindergarten.

Grand Master Rhee has written: "I remember the book "All I Really Need to Know I Learned in Kindergarten" by Robert Fulghum. We learn nothing but character building in kindergarten. Robert Fulghum is saying that if you learned to be absolutely honest, you learned everything. Thomas Jefferson wrote."

"The first chapter in the book of wisdom is honesty." *Thomas Jefferson*

Thomas Jefferson is saying that if you learned to be absolutely honest, you are a man of wisdom.

"Although deception is the only problem, there are exceptions, sometimes called 'white lies.' For example, Miss Shim Chung was the beautiful daughter of a very poor blind man in ancient Korea. Shim Chung begged for a bowl of rice for her hungry father.

When she took the bowl of rice home for her father, her father asked her, 'Did you eat?' She had not eaten, but she replied, 'Yes, sir.' Isn't that a beautiful lie?"

The martial arts industry not only focuses on the importance of personal discipline, respect, and education, but it also teaches the difference between good and evil as well as character of the mind and heart. Now, I understand why the philosophy of TRUTOPIA has emerged from the heart and mind of Grand Master Rhee and the realization of TRUTOPIA has landed in the hands of martial artists.

In my opinion, Grand Master Rhee has experienced miraculous achievements by living out his passion to prepare for TRUTOPIA. I sincerely hope that he will earn your trust after reading this, a small book with giant contents.

Grand Master Jhoon Rhee began his Taekwondo training at the age of 14, in the Chung Do Kwan studio in Seoul, Korea. This picture was taken when Grand Master Rhee was promoted to eighth degree white belt in 1948. Please see the circle in the left front row.

21 Miraculous Achievements Toward the Coming of TRUTOPIA

Miraculous Achievement #1

Washington, DC first, but soon the entire world learns about Taekwondo.

In Washington, DC in 1962, Grand Master Rhee wrote letters to most of the ambassadors from around the world who were serving in the Capital. He informed these dignitaries about the opening of the Jhoon Rhee Taekwondo School at 2035 K Street NW, Washington, DC. He captured their attention by promising he would guarantee their children's character education and help them make all A's and B's in their academic studies. Without his global vision for TRUTOPIA, he wouldn't have thought of such an idea.

When Grand Master Rhee placed two small advertisements in The Washington Post sports page, he could not believe how often the phone rang all day with people asking for more information about tuition and class times. Over 200 people attended the opening day to see his one-man Taekwondo demonstrations done in less than 1,000 square feet of studio space.

His Excellency, Ambassador Il-Kwon Chung of the Korean Embassy, was the guest of honor and welcomed the audience. He said: "There is an old Korean saying that goes, 'The smaller a green pepper, the hotter it is.' I was the Chief of Staff of the Korean Army when Grand Master Rhee was working under me as a young army officer. Grand Master Rhee was the smallest but the hottest young man I had..." People enjoyed the joke and applauded with enthusiasm.

Grand Master Rhee broke three one-inch boards with his speed punch. He also broke another three one-inch boards seven feet off the ground with his famous jump kick. Remember, he is only five feet six inches tall. At the end of the day, twelve people signed up on the spot. He had over 30 students within a month. By the end of August, he had 125 enthusiastic students training in the school. So, of course, Grand Master Rhee had to stay in Washington, DC and leave behind his civil engineering degree. He has remained in Washington, DC ever since.

One day, to his surprise, a distinguished looking gentleman walked into his studio and introduced himself to Grand Master Rhee. "Hi! My name is Captain John Fightner of the US Navy, and I am interested in Taekwondo." He continued, "I read a lot about the tough Korean soldiers using Taekwondo in Vietnam." After a ten minute trial lesson, he signed up for classes. The next day, he brought a dozen other Navy officers to join. Grand Master Rhee could not believe his change in fortune. It seemed like just yesterday he was a house boy for a US soldier living in Korea in 1945. And now, he was elevated to be the Taekwondo instructor for a dozen military officers, including three Navy Captains. He thought, "What a contrast in one life!"

Along with the military officers, many foreign ambassadors' children were training with Grand Master Rhee. One of the school's policies was that if children did not make good grades, they could not take the Black Belt test. So children had to study their academics and many of the ambassadors were happy because their children were making good grades. Several ambassadors requested Grand Master Rhee send his instructors to South America and Africa, to teach classes in their homelands.

Grand Master Rhee did not have enough instructors available because he wanted to expand his school operations as quickly as possible in America. So, he had to introduce the ambassadors to his old Taekwondo classmates from Korea. Grand Master Rhee had in mind that Taekwondo would someday be the forerunner for the global TRUTOPIA message.

These Korean instructors settled down around the world in their new home nations and gave demonstrations for neighboring countries, to inspire them to also invite Taekwondo instructors from Korea. Of course, Grand Master Rhee encouraged and directed them to do so. Today there are estimated to be over 60 million Taekwondo brothers and sisters in 189 countries. As you may be aware, Taekwondo is one of only two martial arts accepted in the Olympic Games; the other is Judo.

Taekwondo exported not only self-defense and discipline for youth, but also the Korean language and Korean food such as delicious kimchi. More importantly, many of the instructors became the chief body guards for the kings and presidents of their countries. When Samsung, Hyundai, LG, SK, and other corporations were still in their infant stages in the 1950s and 1960s, these instructors made valuable business connections for them.

Most Korean people are unaware how much Taekwondo instructors have contributed to today's Korean economic success. Taekwondo has the highest brand name value among all Korean businesses around the world. Samsung, Hyundai, LG, and SK are in second place, and kimchi is in third place.

Miraculous Achievement #2

Grand Master Rhee established Taekwondo classes for members of the United States Congress.

Grand Master Rhee's dream has always been to teach members of the US Congress and to enhance the public image of Taekwondo. It seemed like merely wishful thinking. The public image of Taekwondo was very low in Korea in the old times. So he thought it was very important to enhance the image of Taekwondo, to succeed in America. He gave free lessons to many celebrity figures, particularly media reporters, to inform the general public about the true values of Taekwondo. Grand Master Rhee remembered a lesson from his father, Jinhoon Rhee, who used to say: "If your dream is strong enough and long enough, the dream will always come true."

Grand Master Rhee did not know that his dream of teaching members of the US Congress was coming true. One day, his student, Dr. Jose Jones, handed him a front page story published in The Washington Post. The story was about Rep. James Cleveland of New Hampshire, who was mugged and injured near Capitol Hill in April 1965. Grand Master Rhee immediately called Rep. Cleveland's office, to make known that he had a Taekwondo school in DC He expressed his wish to teach him Taekwondo so he could defend himself. He left a message for the Congressman to call back if he was interested in lessons. Grand Master Rhee remembered the old Korean adage: **"Don't wait for an apple to fall into your mouth; climb up the tree to get one."**

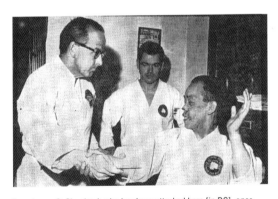

Rep. James C. Cleveland, who has been attacked here [in DC], once with a linoleum knife and once with a letter opener, yesterday learned some Oriental Wisdom. "The safest way with a knife is the further away you are." This pearl came from Jhoon Rhee, who also taught Rep. Cleveland a few Karate tricks. Rep. Cleveland, left, couldn't have been more serious lunging at Mr. Rhee with a letter opener, as fellow Karate expert John Dutcher watches. *Washington Post News photo by Lou Hollie.*

Surprisingly, Grand Master Rhee received a call from the Congressman the next day. Rep. James Cleveland was interested in taking lessons. When he asked Grand Master Rhee for the time and prices for lessons, Grand Master Rhee immediately offered him lessons for free and said he would even go to the Hill to save the Representative's precious time. The Congressman really appreciated the idea and said, "I will ask a few of my colleagues, to see if we could form a class on the Hill."

Then, the Congressman asked, "Why free?" Grand Master Rhee replied, "Sir, I have been grateful for what America did for Korea during the Korean War. I know 34,000 precious young American lives have been sacrificed for a country they never heard of, people they never knew. I wanted to do something to pay back, in my small way, for this American generosity, sir. I fought our common enemies side by side with American soldiers. I often broke into tears whenever I ran into injured American soldiers." He replied, "Thank you, Mr. Rhee."

Jhoon Rhee has never forgotten his gratitude to America for the 34,000 lives sacrificed to protect freedom in Korea. Photo at the Korean War Memorial.

A. It has been 45 years since the first class on the Hill began in the House members' gymnasium on May 6, 1965.

There have been over 350 members of the US Congress who attended his classes during the past 45 years. There are 19 Black Belts among the members. One of his first member students was Vice President Joe Biden. Then, a few years later, NBC's John Chancellor wanted to do a news piece covering a Congressional training session. The session was attended by Senators Ted Stevens and Quentin Burdick, and Representatives Richard Ichord, James Symington, Floyd Spence, and Tom Bevill.

Grand Master Rhee is still teaching the classes three mornings a week. Master Ronnie Kim, one of his assistant instructors, has joined him to teach as well. He misses the classes whenever he travels to spread the TRUTOPIA message, but Master Kim is always there. He has five or six members attending each class.

Another important reason for the Congressional class is that, when Grand Master Rhee declares the Taekwondo philosophy of TRUTOPIA, it may run into objections from the established social structures of today. Without the Global Vision, not many other instructors would have maintained 45 years of teaching free-of-charge. His hope is that the White House and the US Congress will endorse TRUTOPIA, vouching for Grand Master Jhoon Rhee as a patriotic American if he ever faces social objections. (Please, be sure to watch the enclosed DVD.)

Powerful chin strike by Chairwoman Rep. Carolyn Maloney.

Mike Espy, former Secretary of Agriculture, breaking boards.

B. Grand Master Rhee organized high-spirited Republican vs. Democrat sparring matches at a September 14, 1975 tournament in the Washington, DC Armory.

Enthusiasm for Taekwondo training on the Hill ran very high among members of Congress, but no one believed an actual tournament would ever take place.

The Republican Party was represented by Senator Ted Stevens of Alaska, Rep. Floyd Spence of South Carolina, and Rep. Bill Gradison, Jr. of Ohio. The Democratic Party was represented by Senator Quentin Burdick of North Dakota, Rep. Tom Bevill of Alabama, and Delegate Walter Fauntroy of Washington, DC.

The matches ended in a draw, but the event created a positive image of Taekwondo. The event was held before a live audience of over 5,000 people, aired on national television, and was covered by the foreign press. Impressively, the event was also featured as the cover story of Parade magazine, with its weekly circulation of 30 million. Suddenly, this Korean activity was one of the fastest-growing and most popular new American sports.

Frank Gannon—
He's Researching
Nixon's Autobiography
by Lloyd Shearer

The Big Bout in Congress
by Jack Anderson

cover photo: **Senators Quentin Burdick (l) and Ted Stevens Come Out Fighting**

Senator Quentin Burdick of N. Dakota vs. Senator Ted Stevens of Alaska.

Miraculous Achievement #3

Grand Master Rhee choreographed the first Martial Arts Ballet, "Might for Right," performed to the theme song from the motion picture "Exodus."

In 1968, Grand Master Rhee choreographed the first musical form in martial arts history, called "Might for Right," performed to the theme song from the movie "Exodus." It also included a prose narrative describing the philosophy behind the Martial Arts Ballet. The narrative, "Might for Right," invokes ideas parallel to the Bible, from Genesis to Revelations. The song lasts for two minutes and eighteen seconds; and he timed both the narrative and the choreography to perfectly synchronize with the music.

"Might for Right" has been the motto of the Jhoon Rhee Institute of Taekwondo since its founding in 1962. This motto refers to a theme echoed in history: "right" meant "righteous" and "left" meant "sinister" in languages such as Russian, Spanish, German, Korean, and others. Of course, this doesn't mean that left-handed people are evil. His son, Jimmy Rhee, is left-handed, but Jimmy is certainly a good man.

Here is the Ballet's narrative, written over 40 years ago, in 1968, to describe the Jhoon Rhee Martial Arts philosophy.

"Might For Right"

In the beginning, when the universe was created, the energy of God swept across the great void in a definite direction. Truth, Beauty, and Love (TBL) manifested through all things of His creation. Then He molded His crowning achievements, His beloved children: man and woman.

Since then, one strange element that has remained a mystery crept into the midst of all mankind: the evil force: Deceiving, Ugliness, and Hatred (DUH). Let us make the left hand a symbol of that evil. As the sinister left hand covers the righteous right, so has evil tried to destroy the good, just as Cain murdered Abel at the beginning of history.

From that time on, the history of mankind has known a constant conflict between good and evil, as the righteous right and the sinister left clash against each other. It is our only hope that the absolute power of His Love and our actions can someday bring an eternal end to evil.

There shall be no more Deceiving, no more Ugliness, no more Hatred.
There will come a time when all mankind will live in peace and happiness on this earth.
As Truth, Beauty, and Love cast all the evil elements out of this universe,
so does the righteous right cover the evil left: Might for Right.

Tokyo, Japan (June, 1990)

All Jhoon Rhee Taekwondo students, around the world, are required to pass the test on Martial Arts Ballet performance to their National Anthem, God Bless America, Korean and American National Anthems.

Kiev, Ukraine (Feb. 2001)

Soviet Embassy, Wash. (Dec. 1991)

Moscow (Dec. 1989)

Seoul (Korea)

Kazhakstan (Nov. 1991)

U.S. House Cannon (July, 2001)

Arlington, VA (Oct. 1990)

A. Martial Ballet performed to the National Anthem of the United States is taught in eight nations around the world to promote the American FREEDOM System.

Every movement is synchronized to the beat of the music. For daring to create this new art form, many Taekwondo masters called Grand Master Rhee all kinds of nasty names, such as "Fool Master Jhoon Rhee." Yet today, almost all martial artists practice some kind of musical forms, and all martial arts tournaments feature grand championship competitions in demonstrating them.

Later on, Grand Master Rhee choreographed Martial Ballets to "God Bless America," "The Star Spangled Banner," and the Korean National Anthem. It takes time to teach a song so, obviously, it takes much longer to teach choreographed movements. Today, Martial Ballet to national anthems are taught to all Jhoon Rhee Taekwondo students around the world, to promote patriotism for their countries, the American FREEDOM system, and peace among all peoples of the world.

When an ideal human society is realized, professions which produce nothing will slowly disappear: no soldiers, no police officers, no lawyers, no accountants, no Taekwondo fighters, and many other professions as well. Everyone will be healthy, wealthy, and happy. If you are wealthy, you don't have to work. Then how will you spend all your spare time? Perhaps you will sing, paint, dance, exercise, cook, design dresses or build buildings, and so on. These are the arts that express your love for something, someone, or some idea.

I am sure the ultimate destination of our human society is just such an ideal life for everyone. If God is good, He must have designed a perfect place for the happiness of all His children.

B. A Human American Flag performed the Martial Ballet "God Bless America" on the Mall on July 4, 1982.

Two incredible coincidences:

1. 229 students, representing the American population of 229 million, formed the Human Stars & Stripes; and 206 students, standing for the 206th Independence Day of 1982, added up (229 + 206 = 435) to the exact number of members of the US House of Representatives. Grand Master Rhee did not notice this coincidence until after the event: each student had represented one of the 435 members of the House.

2. The performance time for the God Bless America Martial Ballet on the Mall was 3:00 p.m. in Washington, DC, which was noon in California. At that exact time, on July 4, 1982, President Ronald Reagan was singing the same song, "God Bless America," when the Shuttle Columbia (STS-4) landed at the Edwards Air Force Base in California.

Jhoon Rhee's Human Stars and Stripes created for the 1982 July Fourth event on The Mall.

Miraculous Achievement #4

Grand Master Rhee invented Jhoon Rhee Safety Equipment, the world's first padded gear for safe martial arts training and competition.

In 1969, one of Grand Master Rhee's dear students, Pat Worley, who was also an instructor, got seriously injured during a competition. Being the moral man he is, Grand Master Rhee felt he had to choose to either quit the Taekwondo business or invent gear for the safety of his students and for the industry. Of course, in order to invent martial arts safety equipment, you must know martial arts as well as how to design engineering products. Grand Master Rhee is a civil engineer from the University of Texas as well as an expert in martial arts. He was already fully prepared to create a complete line of safety equipment for all Martial Arts.

Soon Grand Master Rhee invented the Jhoon Rhee line of safety equipment. They were called Safety Face, Safety Glove, Safety Kick, Safety Chest, Safety Shin, Safety Elbow and more. All together he created over twelve US patents and holds patents in 15 other major countries. Most martial artists believe that these inventions saved the martial arts industry and allowed it to grow faster because soon the insurance companies would not insure any school that did not use safety equipment.

Jhoon Rhee's Safety-Face is displayed in New York City's Museum of Modern Art. Master Jhoon Rhee received a surprise letter from the Museum informing him that, along with some of the world's greatest art works, his Safety-Face invention had been selected to be permanently displayed.

During the seventeen years of his patent protection, Grand Master Rhee was financially comfortable enough to expand his school operations to the former Soviet Union. There are over 65 Jhoon Rhee Taekwondo Schools in Russia, Ukraine, Kazakhstan, and Uzbekistan.

Chun Rhee (Grand Master Rhee's son) with a safety helmet, safety glove, and safety chest.

The Museum of Modern Art

Terence Riley
Chief Curator
Department of
Architecture and Design

June 19, 1998

Mr. Jhoon Rhee, Grandmaster
Jhoon Rhee Tae Kwon Do
1120 A. W. Broad Street
Falls Church, VA 22046

Dear Mr. Rhee,

It is my great pleasure to inform you that on April 22, 1998 the Acquisition Committee
for the Department of Architecture and Design agreed to include your "Jhoon Rhee
Safety Face" Mask in the permanent collection.

You will find enclosed the Museum's promotional and publication guidelines. Please
Pay careful attention to them, and do feel free to call us should you have any questions.

This piece made so important contribution to our 1991 exhibition. Modern Masks and
Helmets, and we are delighted that we may now officially add it to our collection.

Sincerely,

Terence Riley
Chief Curator

Miraculous Achievement #5

Grand Master Rhee became an international movie star after the legendary Bruce Lee recommended him to Golden Harvest Films in 1973.

Bruce Lee and Grand Master Jhoon Rhee were special guests who were invited to present martial arts demonstrations at Master Ed Parker's International Karate Championships in Long Beach, California on August 1, 1964. Bruce Lee gave a Kung Fu demonstration, and Grand Master Rhee demonstrated Taekwondo. They both earned mutual respect for each other on a day when each also changed Martial Arts history. Grand Master Rhee was impressed by Bruce Lee's high-quality punching presentation. Bruce Lee was impressed by Grand Master Rhee's Taekwondo kicks.

Ever since then, they became best friends. In those days, they exchanged visits with each other once a year. Grand Master Rhee's house was Bruce Lee's home in Washington, DC and Bruce Lee's house was Grand Master Rhee's home in Los Angeles. Grand Master Rhee learned Bruce Lee's punching techniques and shared his Taekwondo kicks with Bruce Lee. They learned from each other. However, the media in Korea often tried to highlight their fellow Korean as Bruce Lee's teacher, overlooking how they shared knowledge mutually.

Bruce Lee, in Grand Master Rhee's opinion, was a born martial artist. He was the strongest man, pound for pound, that Grand Master Rhee had ever met. People told him that no one had ever beaten Bruce Lee in arm wrestling. Grand Master Rhee had never before seen anyone do two-finger push ups.

Bruce Lee was not an easy person to be close to, but once he trusted a person, he would go out of his way to be helpful. Although he had never even been in a school drama, Grand Master Rhee made a martial arts movie in Hong Kong due to Bruce Lee's recommendation. Grand Master Rhee

Jhoon Rhee visited Bruce Lee in his home in the early 1970s. In this picture, Bruce Lee had just finished a workout.

Bruce Lee and Jhoon Rhee on a LA beach in 1968. Bruce Lee taught Jhoon Rhee his Jeet Kune Do punches, and Jhoon Rhee taught Bruce Lee his Taekwondo kicks.

played the leading role in "When Taekwondo Strikes" in April 1973. The shooting and editing were completed on July 18, 1973. It was really a miracle to him to be an international movie star.

On July 19, 1973, Bruce Lee called Grand Master Rhee from Hong Kong to inform him that the movie had been edited and was ready to be shown to the world. During the editing, Bruce Lee had to argue with the director of the movie not to change Jhoon Rhee's role to second billing. Grand Master Rhee had signed a contract to play the leading role. The very next day, Grand Master Rhee heard the tragic news that Bruce Lee died on July 20, 1973. Grand Master Rhee immediately called his wife, Linda, and confirmed the sad news was true. He was probably the last person in America to talk to the legendary "Little Dragon" before his death.

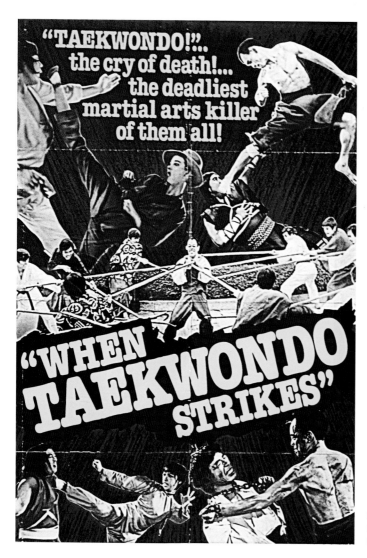

When Taekwondo Strikes is a story about Koreans fighting for independence from Japanese occupation. It was produced in 1973 based on the synopsis written by Master Rhee.

Return of Dragon Masters was produced in Korea in 1980. Also cast were Jeff Smith and Randy Anderson, a son of the late Jack Anderson.

Miraculous Achievement #6

In 1975, Grand Master Rhee became the coach for Boxing Champion Muhammad Ali.

Grand Master Rhee worked as the head coach for World Heavyweight Champion Muhammad Ali before his title-defending match against both the British Boxing Champion Richard Dunn of England and also against the famous Japanese Wrestling Champion Antonio Inoki on June 26, 1976, in Tokyo, Japan.

A. Grand Master Rhee taught a special punch called "Accu-punch" for the title match in Munich, Germany on May 24, 1976. Muhammad Ali knocked Richard Dunn out cold in two minutes and 5 seconds of the fifth round.

Muhammad Ali in the MBC television Show in Korea on June 30, 1976.

The second Dunn was out, the NBC Sportscaster asked Ali, "What kind of punch was that?" Ali announced to the entire world through television, "It was Jhoon Rhee's 'Accu-punch'." Grand Master Rhee could not believe Ali gave him the credit so clearly.

The fight against Antonio Inoki was on June 26, 1976 in Tokyo, Japan. Even though the fight was a draw, it created excitement throughout the world. On June 27, 1976, the day after the fight, Grand Master Rhee was able to persuade Muhammad Ali to visit Korea for his millions of fans. Over twenty people from Ali's camp escorted him to Korea. Greeting the Greatest were over one million fans, packed on both sides of the streets from Kimpo Airport to Seoul, waving the US and Korean flags.

During their visit to Korea, Ali's popularity was at its peak because he had knocked out the giant George Foreman in 1974. Muhammad and his entourage were in Seoul for four days and three nights, during which time Ali made over twelve personal appearances and attended several special events. Grand Master Rhee earned the hearts of his Korean brothers and sisters by bringing Ali to Korea. More Koreans knew of Jhoon Rhee's activities because of this celebrated trip.

Miraculous Achievement #7

Grand Master Rhee was named "Martial Arts Man of the Century" at the US Bicentennial Sports Awards in 1976.

In 1976, America celebrated its Bicentennial Year of Independence. Grand Master Rhee was honored as "Martial Arts Man of the Century." The Washington Touchdown Sports Club selected five sports figures for the Bicentennial Sports Award. The five award recipients were Muhammad Ali as "Boxer of the Century," Wilt Chamberlain as "Basketball Man of the Century," Joe DiMaggio as "Baseball Man of the Century," Jim Brown as "Football Man of the Century," and Grand Master Rhee as "Martial Arts Man of the Century."

Beloved comedian Bob Hope was the Master of Ceremonies who welcomed 2,000 people for a sit-down dinner. Secretary of State Henry Kissinger received the first award as the "Man of the Century." Grand Master Rhee followed Muhammad Ali, to receive his award after Jack Anderson introduced him. Jack was saying how tough Grand Master Rhee was. One of the hottest media debating issues at that time was who would win in a fight between Ali and Chamberlain. In his brief remarks after receiving the award, Grand Master Rhee said, "Mr. Kissinger, I want you to know that your staff members in the US Embassy in Seoul are working very hard and smart to pick the right people to issue visas only to good people like me."

People laughed, and he continued. "There has been a dispute. Who is the greatest, Ali or Chamberlain? You just heard Jack Anderson say who is the greatest. I think Ali and I should settle the dispute for good right here on this stage tonight. Ali, please come out to the stage." The audience was so excited, he continued, "Chamberlain, I don't want you to come out at the same time. Wait until I knock Ali out first."

The audience thought they were going to see the greatest show on Earth! Bob Hope joked, "Well, he must have a hell of jock strap." Grand Master Rhee was very proud.

Another notable event in Korea followed four years later. A new President of Korea, Chun, Doo-Hwan, was inaugurated in 1980. Jack Anderson and Grand Master Rhee were in Seoul at the Inauguration. They were two of Chun's first dinner guests on the day before the Inauguration. Grand Master Rhee is proud to say that he was the first person to sign the Blue House guest book in 1980.

President Chun, Doo-Hwan was invited by President Ronald Reagan to visit America for the Summit Meeting in January 1981. Grand Master Rhee gathered ten bus-loads of Taekwondo students for a Welcome Celebration. The buses waited near the Blair House for four hours, from 9:00 a.m. to 1:00 p.m., because the President's arrival was delayed. Grand Master Rhee had to feed each one of the 500 students a hamburger and soda, which he had not expected. Again, this event was televised nationwide in Korea. It helped set the groundwork for future TRUTOPIA promotions in Korea.

Grand Master Rhee shaking hands with the Master of Ceremonies Bob Hope.

Jhoon Rhee shows his famous sidekick to World Boxing Champion Muhammad Ali at the Deer Lake, Pennsylvania Training Camp in 1976.

Miraculous Achievement #8

Grand Master Rhee served as the Chairman of our Nation's Birthday Celebration for July 4th, 1982.

In 1982, Grand Master Rhee was requested to serve as the Chairman of our Nation's Fourth of July Birthday Celebration. Grand Master Rhee could not believe an Asian American could be the chairman of America's Birthday Celebration. It was as much a miracle to him then as Barack Obama becoming President of the United States is a miracle to him today. Grand Master Rhee accepted the position as quickly as he could before anyone could change their mind.

Grand Master Rhee did everything possible to make it one of the best July Fourth events ever held. He organized an advisory committee with the biggest names he could find from each State. Most of them were from the US Senate and House of Representatives. Grand Master Rhee also contacted one of America's most famous singers, Wayne Newton, for the July Fourth Concert on the Mall, which drew a crowd of nearly a million people. Wayne Newton shook hands with Grand Master Rhee; and the Human Flag was the first group to lead the Grand Parade.

In order to show his love for America, and for what America did for his motherland, Korea, during the Korean War, Grand Master Rhee donated $15,000 for the famous July Fourth fireworks display. Grand Master Rhee also organized a huge human Stars & Stripes formation with his Taekwondo students wearing red, white, and blue uniforms. Two hundred twenty nine students represented the American population of 229 million, and 206 additional students stood for the 206th American Independence Day. With this formation, they marched as the leading group in the Parade, and later performed "God Bless America," a Martial Ballet, along with the Human Flag formation on the Mall. The Jhoon Rhee Parade group won First Prize among 126 Parade Groups competing.

God Bless America performance on the Mall.

Miraculous Achievement #9

Grand Master Rhee conducted the first Martial Arts School Business and Philosophy Seminar to revive the industry in 1985.

Grand Master Rhee began his martial arts school business in 1962 in Washington, DC. He was so successful that he was able to purchase a home in Arlington, Virginia in five years for $60,000.00 in 1967. It seemed like a mansion to him at that time. A few days before he bought the house, he showed a photograph to his assistant instructor, Jack Dutcher, a tough former US Marine, to see his reaction. Dutcher said, "It is too big for you. People will think you're a Chinese houseboy." Jack always loved to tease his master instructor.

Sure enough, when Grand Master Rhee was mowing the lawn one sunny Sunday morning, a gentleman passing by in a black Cadillac convertible stopped his car and shouted, "Say, boy! How much an hour do you charge?" Master Rhee replied: "Nothing, sir, but I get to share the master bedroom with the madam who owns the house." The man drove away quietly.

Grand Master Rhee was one of very few martial artists who believed in heavy advertising in the 1960s. He spent a lot on the TV Guide section of The Washington Post and also on television advertising using the theme "Nobody Bothers Me." The jingle is still recognized today and can be seen on YouTube. He was known as one of the most successful martial arts school operators in the country.

In the 1980s, Grand Master Rhee was very concerned with the declining popularity of martial arts. Nobody thought of providing martial arts business seminars for struggling school owners. Somehow, most instructors had been influenced by their old Asian masters to feel that making money with martial arts is committing some sort of a crime. They were proud to say, "I teach martial arts for free." Master Rhee always asked them, "Do you think what you teach has no value?" He was one of a few who made his teaching Taekwondo very professional and was proud to do so.

Grand Master Rhee announced the first Martial Arts Business Seminar to be conducted in Fort Worth, Texas from July 4-6, 1985. The seminar began at 2:00 p.m. on Friday, went until midnight, then ran from 6:00 a.m. to midnight on Saturday, and from 6:00 a.m. to 5:00 p.m. on Sunday. There were thirty students attending: Pat Burleson, the owner of the Studio, Al Garza, H. K. Lee, George Menshew, Steve Oliver, Ishmael Robles, Jose Santamaria, and other notables.

The seminars became so popular that Grand Master Rhee conducted monthly seminars for several years. Those who attended these seminars and are still active in the martial arts industry are Pat Burleson, Dennis Brown, Tom Callos, Joon Chung, Azhakh Fariborz, Jim Harrison,

David Kovar, Soojin Lee, Ernie Reyes, Simon & Philip Rhee, Jose Santamaria, Don Wilson and many others. Many of the seminar graduates were soon grossing one million dollars or more per year, starting from less than $100,000. Grand Master Rhee has always lived by Ben Franklin's philosophy:

"The most acceptable service we render to Him is in doing good to His other children."
Ben Franklin

You can see why Grand Master Rhee has devoted himself to the toughest task in history, creating TRUTOPIA, where everyone is healthy, wealthy, and happy. In his seminars, Grand Master Rhee covered not only how to do business, but also how to live life, based on the martial art philosophy. Most of the business success enjoyed by seminar attendees was directly proportional to the degree they were motivated to live an honorable life. Master Tom Callos is a good example. The Grand Master remembers reading one of his articles, which said: "I really did not learn much on business technique, but I was pumped up in life by his Martial Arts Action Philosophy."

Born To Be Healthy, Wealthy, & Happy Seminar Three-Day Schedule

Hours	Friday	Saturday	Sunday
06:00		Jhoon Rhee Daily Dozen	Jhoon Rhee Daily Dozen
07:00		Breakfast	Breakfast
08:00		Martial Arts Business	Martial Arts Business
09:00		Universal Values of Life	10021 Club Campaign
10:00		Martial Arts Business	Martial Arts Business
11:00		Martial Arts Training	Martial Arts Training
Noon	Martial Arts Business	Martial Arts Business	
13:00		LUNCH	LUNCH
14:00	Registration	US Founding Fathers	Q & A
15:00	Video Showing	Martial Arts Business	Certificate Award
16:00	7 Qualities of a Champion	Martial Arts Training	End of Seminar
17:00	6 Steps of MA Business	Martial Arts Business	
18:00	DINNER	DINNER	
19:00	Universal Purpose of Life	Power of VISION	
20:00	Martial Arts Business	Martial Arts Business	
21:00	Martial Arts Training	Martial Arts Training	
22:00	Martial Arts Business	Martial Arts Business	
23:00	Martial Arts Training	Martial Arts Training	
24:00	Bed Time	Bed Time	

Please note that in addition to the schedule above, five hours of philosophy were taught.

Miraculous Achievement #10

Grand Master Rhee created The National Teacher Appreciation Day, which was signed by President Ronald Reagan on October 16, 1986.

A. National Teacher Appreciation Day

Grand Master Rhee had been concerned with academic and moral decline among elementary school students. He decided to create National Teacher Appreciation Day by persuading 218 law makers to do something about the problem. Grand Master Rhee talked to each member whom he had met through Taekwondo. The Honorable E. Clay Shaw of Florida agreed to sponsor the National Teacher Appreciation Day Bill in the US Congress.

Grand Master Rhee thought of conducting an annual event at the end of each school year during which students could express their appreciation to their teachers by presenting flowers or letters of kind words. These events would give teachers the opportunity to appreciate their students and to do a better job teaching in the future years. The National Teacher Appreciation Day was passed by the House and Senate, the Bill H.J. RES. 635 on January 28, 1986. It was signed by President Ronald Reagan on October 16, 1986.

B. Annual essay and speech contest entitled, "Why I Appreciate My Teachers."

The Annual National Teacher Appreciation Day (ANTAD) program was planned. The program is to conduct an annual essay and speech contest entitled, "Why I Appreciate My Teachers." The proposed ANTAD essay should be completed by the end of April of each year. Then, the final eight students from 50 State Champions will be selected for a speech contest on national television on the first Friday in May of each year.

The Annual National Teacher Appreciation Day (ANTAD) Foundation planned to award scholarship funds to the winners from each state and the national champion, totaling up to one million dollars annually. These extraordinary cash prizes will serve to elevate the visibility of this essay contest and its winners—inspiring teachers, parents, and students to work together to help our youth achieve their potential, to grow up to be confident, happy, contributing members of society.

This proposal is an appeal to the United States Congress to amend H.J. RES. 635 to approve the Annual National Teacher Appreciation Day Essay Contest as an annual activity. Grand Master Rhee appreciated the Honorable E. Clay Shaw of Florida for sponsoring the bill and working to amend the bill to establish the essay contest as an annual celebration. Unfortunately, it was not amended.

Jhoon Rhee shaking hands with President Reagan. Jhoon Rhee served as
a Commissioner on Vocational Education during the Reagan Administration.

THE WHITE HOUSE

WASHINGTON

November 25, 1986

Dear Clay:

On October 16, 1986, I was pleased to sign into
law House Joint Resolution 635, which designates
the school year of September 1986 through May 1987
as the "National Year of the Teacher" and designates
January 28, 1987, as "National Teacher Appreciation
Day."

This legislation commemorates the contributions
of Christa McAuliffe, our first teacher-astronaut,
and through her the efforts of all teachers, for
their selfless commitment to the education and
fulfillment of our Nation's youth. It is a small
but fitting tribute to those individuals who
dedicate their lives to the goal of instilling
the quest for knowledge and excellence in the
minds and hearts of our country's future -- our
youth.

In recognition of your leadership and sponsorship
of the legislation, I am pleased to present you
with the enclosed pen commemorating the signing
into law of House Joint Resolution 635.

Sincerely,

Ronald Reagan

The Honorable E. Clay Shaw, Jr.
House of Representatives
Washington, D.C. 20515

UNITED STATES OF AMERICA

Congressional Record

PROCEEDINGS AND DEBATES OF THE 99th CONGRESS

SECOND SESSION

VOLUME 132—PART 20

OCTOBER 3, 1986 TO OCTOBER 8, 1986

(PAGES 28211 TO 29849)

TEACHER APPRECIATION

HON. E. CLAY SHAW, JR.
OF FLORIDA
IN THE HOUSE OF REPRESENTATIVES

Monday, October 6, 1986

Mr. SHAW. Mr. Speaker, I introduced House Joint Resolution 635, a resolution that recognizes and honors our Nation's teachers. This resolution was inspired both by Jhoon Rhee, founder of the Institute of Tae Kwon Do, Inc., who has written an excellent essay entitled "Let's Honor Our Teachers by Observing a Teacher's Day," and by Christa McAuliffe the schoolteacher who was a member of the crew for the space shuttle *Challenger*.

In his essay, Jhoon Rhee suggests that the basic principle of respect for teachers, to be embodied in a teacher's day, would restore discipline in our Nation's classrooms. Christa McAuliffe brought the love of learning and the yearning for knowledge to life in the hearts of our Nation's children by her endeavor to become the first teacher in space.

As this teacher appreciation resolution is currently on its way to the White House for signature, I believe this is an appropriate time to share an excerpt from Jhoon Rhee's inspirational essay with my colleagues:

We all remember from childhood that from those teachers whom we respected the most, we learned the most. Nobody wants to learn from someone for whom they have no respect. In this observation, the first foundation for learning is the student's respect for the teacher . . . America only needs to instill discipline in their children once again. The school teachers have to be motivated through more respect and proper social recognition, which in turn will influence students to once again respect their teachers.

Grand Master Rhee volunteered to conduct the "Joy of Discipline" program in 1988 at Amidon and Bowen elementary schools in Southwest Washington through an introduction by Secretary William Bennett of the US Department of Education. The program was widely credited with improving student's self-discipline and self-esteem. The program was expanded to seven additional elementary schools in the District in the fall of 1990.

Amidon Elementary School students in the"Joy of Discipline"Program.

According to Mrs. Pauline Hamlette, Principal of Amidon Elementary School, the "Joy of Discipline" program has produced dramatic improvements in classroom discipline and raised students self-esteem at Amidon. "We don't have a lot of disciplinary problems with these students because the program serves as a vehicle to build self-discipline and a positive self-image," she stated. "It also fosters creativity that allows students to relate better to each other and express themselves in a different manner. Once they enter the program, they perform better in the classroom."

C. Visit to the Moscow City Council of Education

Dr. Constance R. Clark, the Assistant Superintendent for Elementary and Early Childhood Education of the DC Public Schools, loved the "Joy of Discipline" program. Grand Master Rhee proposed to Dr. Clark a trip to visit the Moscow City Council of Education. She agreed to take a few of her principals to visit Moscow because she thought it would be a good experience for them.

Grand Master Rhee and his student Mr. Charles Scott, of Charles Scott Insurance Company, financed the trip. Dr. Constance R. Clark headed a delegation to Moscow consisting of eight principals of the Washington, DC Public Schools. They were hosted by Dr. Ernest Bakirov, Chairman of the Moscow City Council of Education, in Moscow. They joined 80 Moscow principals in a two-day martial arts "Joy of Discipline" program conducted by Grand Master Rhee, Master Kenneth Carlson, and Master Kevin Gilday, a graduate from the Wharton School of Business specializing in Third World development. The new Moscow program has been modeled after the Jhoon Rhee "Joy of Discipline" program.

Pictured during a visit to the Moscow City Council of Education to promote the "Joy of Discipline" program conducted by Master Jhoon Rhee are Dr. Constance R. Clark, Washington, DC Public School System Assistant Superintendent (center); Master Jhoon Rhee (left); Pauline Hamlette, Principal of Amidon Elementary School (left of Master Rhee) and Ernest Bakirov, Moscow Public School Superintendent, (right of Master Rhee).

D. "Joy of Discipline"

"This is a unique opportunity to establish a cooperative relationship between public schools in Washington and Moscow," Dr. Clark commented. "We have much to learn from each other, and I am delighted that Master Rhee and the Charles Scott Insurance Company have made it possible for us to meet with Soviet teachers and school officials, to visit their schools and to compare educational techniques with our Soviet counterparts." Dr. Clark announced that the DC Schools will pilot the "Joy of Discipline" program.

The central themes of the"Joy of Discipline"are as follows:

"If all men were angels, no government would be necessary." *James Madison*

"The first chapter in the book of wisdom is honesty." *Thomas Jefferson*

"A teacher affects eternity; he can never tell where his influences stops." *Henry Adams*

Miraculous Achievement #11

Grand Master Rhee, in 1989, persuaded the USSR Minister of Sports, Anatoly Kolesov, to legalize all martial arts activities in the USSR.

Mr. Charles Sutherland, the president of the Washington Film Company, called Grand Master Rhee on November 12, 1989, suggesting they perform in Moscow the Martial Arts Ballet "Marriage of East and West" done to Beethoven's 5th Symphony. Mr. Sutherland had been a Black Belt student of Grand Master Rhee for the last seven years. The Grand Master could not believe he was so fortunate as to be offered such a unique opportunity. He immediately began to choreograph a Martial Arts Ballet to the Soviet National Anthem, which he named "Mikhail Gorbachev" to honor his Perestroika and Glasnost policies of openness and honesty. Grand Master Rhee and four of his students practiced "Mikhail Gorbachev" for two solid weeks.

Mr. Sutherland called Grand Master Rhee from Moscow to inform him that he could not perform a Martial Arts Ballet done to the Soviet National Anthem because they did not know what reaction to expect from government authorities. Grand Master Rhee told Mr. Sutherland that he would ask the Soviet Embassy to show "Mikhail Gorbachev" performed by Soviet Embassy children, via Soviet television, prior to his arrival to Moscow. Grand Master Rhee knew the Soviet people would be thrilled to hear their National Anthem being played by a Jhoon Rhee Taekwondo School in America. As he had expected, performances of both nation's National Anthems happened during their mission to Moscow.

He took his daughter Meme, 21, and students Andrew, 15, Kehillian, 13, and Mike Garcia, seven, to perform. The group arrived in Moscow on December 14, 1989. Grand Master Rhee could not believe he was in Moscow, to most Americans an unreachable city at that time. Moscow was cold and white with snow. Grand Master Rhee was shocked to witness their poor standard of living. He could not believe that an average wage was less than $100.00 per month. The Grand Master himself was making over $10,000 a month. It reminded him of Korea, where he grew up; Korea was even worse.

On his arrival at a hotel in Moscow on December 14, Grand Master Rhee was greeted by a stranger, Mr. Ilya Gouliev, a 4th degree black belt in Japanese Karate and President of The Soviet Association of Martial Arts. Mr. Gouliev lived in New York City for six years and is the son of a Soviet Diplomat from the early 1960s. He spoke almost perfect English. He knew of Grand Master Rhee through different magazine articles. He volunteered to be Grand Master Rhee's interpreter during his stay in Moscow. He accompanied Grand Master Rhee everywhere in Moscow and Leningrad.

On December 18, 1989, Grand Master Rhee and his students were taken to Rozier Hotel. There, before an audience of 3,000, they performed the Martial Arts Ballet Meegook, meaning "America," done to the American National Anthem, and "Mikhail Gorbachev" done to the National Anthem of the Soviet Union as a way of celebrating Gorbachev's Perestroika and Glasnost policies. US Senator and Mrs. James Jeffords had joined in the trip and on that occasion gave an encouraging speech. The audience received the entire presentation with great enthusiasm.

Grand Master Rhee's team also performed "The Marriage of East & West" to Beethoven's 5th Symphony and then did a comedy piece to the movie theme of "Chariots of Fire," much to the delight of the audience. This show was scheduled to be seen in America on Entertainment Tonight at a later date. The Bush-Gorbachev Submit at Malta, on December 16 and 17, 1989, was followed by the first-time-ever presentation of the Star Spangled Banner in the Soviet Union on December 18, 1989.

The event was very successful and was followed by a reception attended by many dignitaries and covered by reporters from television, newspapers, and magazines. Grand Master Rhee was interviewed by at least a dozen reporters including the Soviet TASS news agency and Izvestia. Then, at 11:30 p.m., the team took a night train to Leningrad and arrived there at 7:00 a.m. the next morning, on December 19, 1989. They all went to a concert hall at 10:00 a.m. to perform another successful show similar to the one they had presented in Moscow. The show was followed by another first-class reception, where Grand Master Rhee met many Leningrad reporters.

On December 20, they were given a special tour of the famous Hermitage Museum. It was usually closed on Mondays but an exception was made for them. It was one of the most memorable experiences of their tour. Later in the afternoon, they were also treated to a sightseeing tour. To Grand Master Rhee, the entire city, with its centuries-old castles and churches, was one giant masterpiece of art. He had never expected to see such an old city so beautifully preserved. They, again, took a night train to return to Moscow on December 21, 1989.

On December 21, Grand Master Rhee conducted a martial arts philosophy seminar at the Moscow University for students, members of the Soviet Association of Martial Arts from Leningrad, Georgia, Armenia, and other states by invitation-only from Mr. Gouliev. The seminar lasted for two and half hours, from 4:00 to 6:30 p.m. The seminar was shown on the news the next morning. Then a TV reporter wanted to do a one-hour special show at 6:00 p.m. on the 22nd. This interview was scheduled to be televised on December 28. The performance earlier at the Rozier Hotel for the Soviet Children's Fund was scheduled to be aired on January 7, 1990, which happens to be Russian Christmas Day and also Grand Master Rhee's birthday.

On December 22, Grand Master Rhee had a productive meeting with the officials of the State Sports Committee. Grand Master Rhee met Minister Anatoly Kolesov, the Deputy Minister of Sports of the USSR, and his assistant Mr. Yuri G. Aleksenko to discuss possible legalization of all martial arts as an official Soviet sport.

On December 24, Mr. Gouliev called to inform Grand Master Rhee that the State Sports Committee had passed a new law that officially legalized all Asian martial arts activities in the Soviet Union. Martial arts had been banned in the Soviet Union for years. Grand Master Rhee was told to expect an invitation soon from Mr. Aleksenko to conduct a Martial Arts Philosophy seminar sometime in early 1990.

On December 23, Mr. and Mrs. Gouliev invited Grand Master Rhee and Mr. Sergey Taranov, the sports editor of the National Izvestia Newspapers, to have a dinner meeting. Mr. Sergey Taranov interviewed Grand Master Rhee and wanted to promote the Jhoon Rhee System throughout the entire Soviet Union. The Grand Master emphasized the greater importance of philosophy over punching and kicking. He stressed that martial arts without philosophy is merely street fighting. Unless martial arts builds the character of our youth through his positive program, it would have no significant role in society. An approving, full page story was published a week later.

On December 24, Grand Master Rhee and the team returned home to Washington, DC He was prouder than ever of being an American and appreciated even more the blessing of living in the United States. Mr. Mikhail Gorbachev's historic doctrines of Perestroika and Glasnost had surely opened the hearts and hopes of Soviet people and marked the beginning of a new age with potential wealth, freedom, and happiness throughout the world.

Many of Grand Master Rhee's friends in the US could not believe that he was waving the Soviet Flag to honor their country since he denounced Communism so avidly. Grand Master Rhee himself could not believe it, either. But it was obvious that the world was changing rapidly. The Grand Master had indeed made martial arts history in the Soviet Union. His trip opened the door for three further seminars in 1990 in the Soviet Union. People were so inspired that the Grand Master had no trouble persuading them to also attend an 11-day, 18-hour-a-day seminar held in January 1991.

A. Grand Master Rhee conducted an 11-day, 18-hour-a-day seminar in Moscow from January 9-19, 1991 for 82 Japanese Karate students. And as a result, sixty-five of them changed from Japanese Karate to Jhoon Rhee Taekwondo.

B. Grand Master Rhee conducted an unprecedented 15-hour Q & A Session on the eleventh day.

According to the Grand Master, "I appreciated Mr. Sergey Tsoy, who invited me on his television show as a guest each time I visited Moscow. Thanks to Mr. Sergey Alikhanov and Andrei Palchevski, who organized the 11-day seminar from 6:00 a.m., January 9 to 11:59 p.m., January 19, 1991, with 82 Japanese Karate students." Grand Master Rhee kept three shifts of English translators working six hours each for eleven days. He especially appreciated

Mr. Andrei Palchevski, the chief translator, who spoke better English than most Americans. He was a former member of the KGB of the Soviet government.

Jhoon Rhee, Sergey Tsoy, and Sergey Alikhanov.

Jhoon Rhee and Sergey Taranov, Russian Sports Editor.

Grand Master Rhee left for Moscow for the seminar on his 60th birthday, January 7, 1991. The seminar consisted of five hours of philosophy, five hours of Taekwondo, five hours of martial arts business strategies, and one hour each for three meals per day. On the 11th day, they had a 15-hour Q & A session during which the Grand Master answered over 500 questions. Finally, one of the students asked the famous "Which came first, the chicken or the egg" question. Grand Master Rhee gave four reasons why the egg has to have been the first to be created.

Reason 1: There is no living creature born that grows smaller in size after birth. Try to find any such living creature. Which is smaller – the chicken or the egg?

Reason 2: Everything we create goes from a simpler to a more complicated state. For example, in order to make a car, nuts, bolts, wires, wheels, seats, engine, body, etc. must be made first before assembling them in proper order to create a car. Which is simpler – the chicken or the egg?

Reason 3: When we create a new thing, first we make only one. Writers create only one original manuscript as a model to publish in great quantities; all product makers create only one model to make a mold for mass production. Grand Master Rhee is sure the Creator created one male and copied him. Then it was only necessary to change the gender to make the first female. Isn't it more economical to copy, rather than invent the same thing again? Which is more economical to copy – the chicken or the egg?

Reason 4: When we create something new, we create it for higher value. Let us go into a grocery store and compare the chicken to the egg. If the egg becomes a chicken, it is creating a higher value. However, if the chicken becomes the egg, it is lowering the value. Which has less value – the chicken or the egg?

Based on the above four reasons, now we all know the answer to the eternal question. Obviously, the answer must be, the egg. Later, Grand Master Rhee found out the man who asked the question was a philosophy professor at Moscow University.

By the end of the seminar, five students dropped out but 82 graduated and earned a Jhoon Rhee Black Belt. They all deserved the promotion because they had taken Japanese Karate for at least ten to twenty years, prior to the seminar. After the long years of training, they were still wearing white belts, for there was no one to promote them, and they were all practicing underground.

C. Grand Master Rhee created 65 Jhoon Rhee Taekwondo Schools in eleven days in the USSR.

When he asked for students who wished to operate the Jhoon Rhee System when they returned to their homes, all 65 instructors present, who already owned Karate schools, raised their hands.

This means that Grand Master Rhee created 65 new Jhoon Rhee Taekwondo Schools in 11 days with his concentrated efforts in the more remote lands of the Soviet Union.

The historic 11-Day Seminar from January 9-19, 1991 was followed by a three-hour concert to celebrate the Seminar, starring the famous singer Oleg Gazmanov performing in the Moscow Youth Palace on the 20th.

Master Alexander Korobov is the Director of the JRI in the CIS.

At a later date, this show was televised nationwide. This was during a period when a few people of the Baltic States were killed by the Soviet Army. When Grand Master Rhee took the microphone to greet the audience, he boldly recalled how American freedom was earned by the Founding Fathers, quoting Patrick Henry's famous words: "Is life so dear, or peace so sweet, as to be purchased at the price of chains and slavery? Forbid it, Almighty God! I know not what course others may take; but as for me, give me liberty or give me death!" Later, Grand Master Rhee found out his quote from Patrick Henry was erased before the show was televised.

Mr. Boris Pyadyshev, the publisher of International Affairs, the official journal of the Soviet Minister of Foreign Affairs, attended the Concert. International Affairs was founded by the former Minister of Foreign Affairs, Mr. Andrei Gromyko. Mr. Boris Pyadyshev took over the position after Andrei Gromyko retired. After the show, Boris Pyadyshev, now the publisher, asked Grand Master Rhee to write an article about his philosophy, "Happyism", for the journal. Grand Master Rhee agreed. In the February 1991 issue of International Affairs of the Gorbachev Administration, he courageously declared that the Soviet style of Communism would never work.

Grand Master Rhee wrote: "The Communism in the Soviet Union, over the past 73 years, is not acceptable to me. I think there is more real Communism practiced in the United States. American Senators drive without chauffeurs and use the same grocery stores as ordinary citizens. However, members of the Soviet Dumas have chauffeurs and special shops apart from ordinary citizens. What kind of Communism is that?"

The article continued: "I use the term Communism, but there are points on which I differ from Karl Marx. His idea and theory are excellent, but he overlooked an important point – our basically greedy human nature. I realize why you are worried about the word 'Communism.' I see that the past 73 years have generated enough bitterness over Communism."

Grand Master Rhee assumed that most people in the Gorbachev Administration had read the above article, because he was invited to the office of the Znanie Society on July 15, 1991, soon after the article was published.

Later, Alexander Potemkin, the Cultural Attache of the former USSR Embassy in Washington told an audience of around 100, including several members of the US Congress in 1991, as follows:

"If you ask me who has now the most influence over the Soviet foreign policies today, I will say, it is Master Jhoon Rhee."

Master Alexander Lee is the Director of the Kazakhstan JRI.

Then, he took out the article from his pocket to show to the audience by raising it up, and continued:

"This editorial article was just published in the Soviet magazine, and read by Soviet diplomats, politicians, and high level officials. This article consists of guiding principles, the philosophy of Master Rhee, which applies even to relationships between nations and between the Soviet Union and the United States."

D. **The Editorial Council of** *International Affairs*, **the official journal of USSR foreign affairs, declared Grand Master Rhee the prize winner for the best material published in 1991 for his article on "Happyism."**

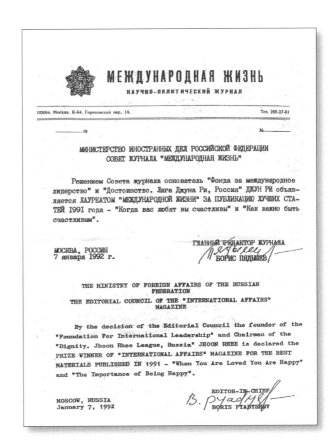

E. **Dr. Vladimir Kudinov, the first vice chairman of the Soviet Znanie Society, met with Grand Master Rhee to discuss the future of the USSR.**

The Znanie Society was responsible for teaching and promoting the ideology of Communism in the USSR and around the world. Ambassador Boris Pyadyshev took Grand Master Rhee to Dr. Vladimir Kudinov, the first vice chairman of the Znanie Society.

Mr. Kudinov explained that the Society was a network organization throughout the 15 republics. He was interested in organizing Grand Master Rhee's tour through all 15 republics, to conduct his seminars on "Happyism." Grand Master Rhee was surprised by this invitation. He felt that he almost put two superpowers, the US and USSR, together as one powerful ally. This was by far the greatest miracle of all. It was too good to be true. Grand Master Rhee told Mr. Kudinov that the real true Communism is the original Creator's design for a happy human society, but greedy human natures must be changed through an effective conscience education. Then the True Communism or TRUTOPIA (True Utopia) will be an automatic reality.

Grand Master Rhee was so excited to motivate everyone with this breaking historical news. Ambassador Pyadyshev told Grand Master Rhee to follow up with Dr. Kudinov when and how he would schedule Grand Master Rhee's return for the "Happyism" or TRUTOPIA seminars. Obviously, most members of the Communist Party must have read the article, because the article won the 1991 Article of the Year Award.

Grand Master Rhee promised Mr. Kudinov he would return to Moscow in 45 days, on September 1, 1991, to conduct lectures for members of the Znanie Society. He bought a round-trip ticket from Washington to Moscow on August 20, in preparation for the trip and was looking forward to the exciting events waiting for him in the USSR. However, his excitement turned to disappointment when the Gorbachev Administration was over-thrown by Boris Yeltsin on August 25, 1991.

Miraculous Achievement #12

In 1999 and 2000, when Bob Hope retired, Grand Master Rhee was invited to take over the beloved comedian's famous USO Show in Korea.

The Grand Master was delighted and honored to accept the offer. He has always been grateful to America, particularly to US soldiers. For their entertainment, Grand Master Rhee's team performed Taekwondo shows in Yongsan and Ohsan. When the soldiers saw Congressman Bob Livingston and Secretary of Agriculture Mike Espy in uniform and breaking boards in 1999, and Congressmen Toby Roth and Jesse Jackson, Jr. in 2000, they gave them a standing ovation. The troops never thought members of Congress were taking Taekwondo so seriously.

The Korean Army Parachute Troop gave a spectacular parachute air show for Grand Master Rhee's American Taekwondo group at the Parachute Division Headquarters in Seoul. When the troopers landed, they put on their own Taekwondo demonstrations against simulated enemies.

Rep. Bob Livingston and the Jhoon Rhee group enjoying a spectacular parachute demonstration by the Korean Army Parachute Brigade in Seoul, Korea.

Miraculous Achievement #13

Grand Master Rhee and world-famous model Cheryl Tiegs were featured on the cover of the March 16, 1997 issue of Parade magazine.

It was truly an honor for the Grand Master to be on the cover of Parade, the most popular publication in the world, with a weekly circulation of over 30 million copies nationwide.

Mr. Ira Yoffe, Parade's director of design, the world-famous model Cheryl Tiegs, and the Father of Taekwondo in the Western Hemisphere, Grand Master Jhoon Rhee on March 16, 1997.

US Speaker Newt Gingrich and Rep. Bob Livingston were invited to visit by President Kim, Young Sam of Korea. Mr. Gingrich requested President Kim pose for a photo with him holding Parade in the Blue House on March 18, 1997.

Miraculous Achievement #14

Grand Master Rhee performed a Harmonica Concerto with the Washington Symphony Orchestra at the French embassy in 2000 and 2005.

Grand Master Rhee has trained in Taekwondo for 65 years and is still training. At the age of six, he also started playing harmonica. He has played for over 70 years and is still playing. The Grand Master served as a Board Member of the Washington Symphony Orchestra until 2002. When the Orchestra needed a fund-raiser, he volunteered to do a Harmonica Concerto in the French Embassy Auditorium in January 2000. They sold 300 tickets or full capacity at $100 per ticket and raised a total of $30,000. Grand Master used eight harmonicas of different keys to play "Blue Danube" by John Strauss.

Grand Master Rhee did not want people to think martial arts is just punching and kicking; he wanted to project a more artistic image for the martial arts. The Harmonica Concerto in Washington, DC was televised in Seoul as a news piece. In 2005, the Seoul Royal Symphony Orchestra asked Grand Master Rhee to perform a Harmonica Concerto during a March 30, 2005 broadcast from the KBS Music Hall.

Grand Master Rhee foresees everyone pursuing some sort of art in his vision of TRUTOPIA. TRUTOPIA will be a perfect global society of performing artists. He feels people were born to perform arts, not to work. We know cooking food, sewing dresses, building houses, and creating useful things are all arts, like music and painting. All other professions are by-products of deceivers, against whom we have to be on guard because, for now, there is no trust among people.

Jhoon Rhee and his brother Sam presenting the Harmonica Concerto at the Korean Broadcasting System (KBS television) Music Hall on March 30, 2005 in Seoul, Korea.

If all people are good, why do we need lawyers, police, soldiers?

"**Politics are divine sciences after all. The science of government it is my duty to study... I must study politics and war, that our sons may have liberty to study mathematics and philosophy. Our sons ought to study mathematics and philosophy, geography, natural history... commerce and agriculture in order to give their children a right to study painting, poetry, music, architecture, statuary, tapestry and porcelain.**" *John Adams*

Miraculous Achievement #15

Grand Master Rhee was named one of 203 most outstanding American immigrants in US history, along with Albert Einstein.

Grand Master Rhee was the only Korean American selected as one of "The 203 Outstanding American Immigrants in US History" in 2000. Grand Master Rhee found out the news through a Korean newspaper article sent from New York by his brother Sam.

The 203 Outstanding American Immigrants were selected by the US Immigration and Naturalization Services along with the National Immigration Forum. The list included Albert Einstein, Alexander Graham Bell, Henry Kissinger, Jhoon Rhee, and 199 others.

He called the National Immigration Forum and requested a copy of the list. He received the list as shown on page 56, which listed only 21 names. Noticing Albert Einstein and Alexander Graham Bell were missing, his conclusion was that they gave him only the list of those who were still living as of the year 2000.

IMMIGRANTS IN THE NEWS

The following list contains the names of first generation immigrants
who left their homelands to reside in the United States.
The contributions of these and other immigrants have enriched
our culture, advanced our sciences, and inspired
us throughout the years.

Two of the most famous men deceased are
• Albert Einstein and • Alexander Graham Bell.

Other immigrants listed are still active:

• Madeleine Albright, US Secretary of State (Czechoslovakia) • Liz Claiborne,
fashion designer (Belgium) • Oscar de la Renta, fashion designer (Dominican
Republic) • John Kenneth Galbraith, economist/presidential advisor (Canada)
• Peter Jennings, network television anchor (Canada) • Henry Kissinger,
former Secretary of State (Germany) • Ted Koppel, network television anchor,
Nightline (England) • Yo-Yo Ma, concert cellist (France – Chinese descent)
• Zubin Mehta, conductor (India) • Yoko Ono, vocalist/songwriter (Japan) •
Seiji Ozawa, conductor (China – Japanese descent) • Itzhak Perlman, violinist
(Israel) • Sidney Poitier, Academy Award-winning actor (Bahamas) • Andre
Previn, pianist/conductor/composer (Germany) • Anthony Quinn, Academy
Award-winning actor (Mexico) • **Jhoon Goo Rhee**, Taekwondo expert (Korea)
• Arnold Schwarzenegger, actor/body builder (Austria) • Elizabeth Taylor,
Academy Award-winning actress (Britain) • Elie Wiesel, author/Nobel Prize
winner for Peace/Holocaust survivor (Romania)

Prepared February 1999 by the National Immigration Forum
220 I Street, NE #220, Washington, DC 20002-4362
Tel: 202-544-0004 • Fax: 202-544-1905

Miraculous Achievement #16

Mayor Anthony Williams of Washington, DC declared June 28, 2003 as Jhoon Rhee Day.

Grand Master Rhee has been teaching members of the US Congress Taekwondo for 45 years as a volunteer. In 2003, Anthony Williams, the Mayor of Washington, DC, declared June 28 to be Jhoon Rhee Day. The first Jhoon Rhee Taekwondo School was founded on June 28, 1962. That date has always been celebrated by Jhoon Rhee Taekwondo schools. Korea sent a group of 18 famous singers to perform at a Peace Concert at RFK Stadium on June 28, 2004. The City wanted to commemorate his 40th anniversary, two years late, in 2004. An estimated 30,000 DC, Maryland, and Virginia residents attended the event. Grand Master Rhee was told he was the first Asian to receive this recognition.

Jhoon Rhee Day

June 28, 2003

A PROCLAMATION BY THE MAYOR OF THE DISTRICT OF COLUMBIA

WHEREAS, its been almost a half-century since Grand Master Jhoon Rhee introduced Tae Kwon Doe to the United States; and

WHEREAS, on June 28, 1962, Jhoon Rhee opened the first professional Tae Kwon Doe School in Washington, D.C. and in 1989, was the first person to introduce Tae Kwon Doe in the former USSR; and

WHEREAS, this event celebrates the 40th anniversary of Jhoon Rhee Tae Kwon Do in the Capital area; and

WHEREAS, in honor of Master Rhee's success, family, friends and students from all over the world will join in a special tribute to honor him for his past achievements.

NOW, THEREFORE, I, THE MAYOR OF THE DISTRICT OF COLUMBIA, do hereby proclaim June 28, 2003, as "JHOON RHEE DAY" in Washington, D.C., and call upon all the residents of this great city to join me in recognizing this distinguished gentleman and wish him continued success.

Anthony A. Williams
Mayor, District of Columbia

Miraculous Achievement #17

Grand Master Rhee presented a speech at the United Nations on April 10, 2007.

Grand Master Rhee was invited by Mrs. Jenny Hou, one of his friends, to present a speech at a Chinese New Year Party for Wall Street dignitaries. Grand Master Rhee thought it would be an interesting event. Dr. Steve Einstein, a grandson of Albert Einstein, and Vice Ambassador Joon Oh of the Korean United Nations Mission attended the party. Grand Master Rhee's speech made such an impact on the Vice Ambassador that he was invited to speak at the United Nations.

Ambassador Joon Oh arranged for Grand Master Rhee to speak at the United Nations on April 10, 2007, before an audience of 200 Ambassadors, Vice Ambassadors, and their staff members. The speech was entitled "Mending Our Troubled World through a Philosophy of Action." It was taped and edited to be shared with everyone who is interested in Grand Master Rhee's philosophy. (Please visit www.jhoonrhee.com to watch and listen to Grand Master Rhee speaking for 59 minutes at the United Nations). He had given speeches for many government agencies including the US Congress and the White House but never before at the UN.

Dr. Steve Einstein held boards for a breaking demonstration. UN Secretary General Ban, Ki-Moon, Korean UN Ambassador Choi, Young Jin were present.

Miraculous Achievement #18

Grand Master Rhee performed 100 push ups in 62 seconds at the age of 76.

During the UN speech, Grand Master Rhee gave a brief demonstration. He performed 100 push ups in 62 seconds. He did a split stretch, touching his chest to the floor, and broke three unsupported boards with his bare knuckle Accu-punch. He balanced on one foot and stretched his other leg over his head. Most surprisingly, these demonstrations were done after recovering from a stroke on February 11, 2004. It should also be noted that, prior to his stroke, he used to do 100 push ups in 57 seconds.

Over the years, Grand Master Rhee's demonstrations have thrilled audiences worldwide. He first met Bruce Lee at Ed Parker's celebrated 1964 International Karate Championship in Long Beach, California on August 1, 1964. They both went to the Dominican Republic, where Grand Master Rhee scheduled his students' black belt tests in 1970. Bruce Lee gave his amazing demonstration, which the audience loved.

Years later, Grand Master Rhee met self-help author and motivational speaker Tony Robbins when the Grand Master attended one of his seminars. Tony Robbins went on to earn his Jhoon Rhee Black

Belt in eight months, the shortest time ever achieved by any of Grand Master Rhee's many students. Since then, many martial artists have attended Tony's seminars and become his students.

A few photos in memory of Bruce Lee's visit to the Dominican Republic in July 1970: welcoming at the airport; attending my black belt testing; and on a Dominican TV interview show.

When Grand Master Rhee sent a DVD of his United Nations speech to Tony Robbins and Linda Lee, they wrote these encouraging letters.

Linda Lee Cadwell and Jhoon Rhee in Fort Worth, Texas honoring Bruce Lee.

Linda Lee Cadwell
2165 Bluestem Lane
Boise, Idaho 83706

July 10, 2007

My dear friend Grandmaster Jhoon Goo,

I am proud to call you my friend. Your speech to the United Nations was truly inspirational. I will save it and show it to my children and grandchildren that they might learn the Philosophy of Action that you have shared with the world.

I know you have studied, not only with your brain and body, but also with your heart, to know what is important to the human condition. The Seven Qualities of a Champion are truisms that will lead to that perfect quality of life where Love, Beauty and Truth will prevail. I congratulate you on your deep insights into the true goal of a human being to attain happiness.

I believe that the new part of your message, which is to "Love One Another", will offer hope to the peoples of the world who struggle because of religious divisiveness. What a more loving, beautiful and honest world it would be if there could be agreement on this one principle.

In addition to the heart of your message and the knowledge of scientific facts, your physical skills continue to amaze. Your recovery from the stroke has been phenomenal. I am inspired to do my 30 minutes of stretching every evening in front of the TV news.

Sometimes I wonder what "good thing" came out of Bruce and Brandon leaving us so early. Then, when I read letters from people all over the world who have been inspired by their example, I think of your message to parents that we must lead by example, and I think that is what my husband and son did. Bruce Lee is looking down upon you in appreciation of your tireless efforts to help people find happiness. We are all grateful for the long life you have had and will continue to have for decades to come.

You are a very good speaker, not only getting your message across, but injecting humor and entertainment into your speech as well. It is no surprise you are invited to speak all over the world. I wish that your good works will reach the far corners of the earth and will touch the hearts of people in conflict.

Health and happiness,
Linda

LEADERSHIP
NEGOTIATION
PEAK PERFORMANCE

ANTHONY ROBBINS
C O M P A N I E S

May 29, 2007

Dear Jhoon Rhee,

My dear friend! I've missed hearing from you. Both of our lives are so busy, working hard to create a happier and healthier world. I want you to know, I think of you often, and I was thrilled to receive the DVD of your speech on Mending Our Troubled World, with the philosophy of action. You are as vibrant and strong, and beautiful a soul as ever, Master. So often, when I think of doing what is right, I think of your philosophy of doing right. Glad to see the world is still being touched by you.

If you go to my website and see any dates on which you could come to a seminar as my guest, know that you're always welcome.

Also, I have no criticisms of such a fine speech. Please continue touching the world.

Love, Your Friend, Fan, and Student,
Tony Robbins

P.S. I'm enclosing a video iPod with some of my more recent material. Someday, you'll have to meet my wife, Sage ☺

Tony Robbins receiving a Black Belt after passing a test including breaking four one-inch boards and demonstrating other self-defense techniques at his two-week seminar in Maui, Hawaii on July 4, 1989.

Miraculous Achievement #19

Grand Master Rhee received the Russian International Peace Award in Moscow on April 26, 2007.

UN Secretary General Ki-Moon Ban and Grand Master Rhee were awarded the Russian International Peace Award by the Award Committee in Moscow on April 26, 2007. One of the recipients of the Award in 2006 was the Honorable Mikhail Gorbachev, former President of the Soviet Union. He is among the real visionaries and revolutionaries of the 20th Century. He ended the long-lasting Cold War, an achievement which opened the hearts of people around the world.

Grand Master Rhee briefly spoke of his optimistic belief in the Taekwondo philosophy, TRUTOPIA, at the event. He stated, "The ultimate goal of human society is happiness, not peace. However, peace must come before the happy society. Everyone will be comfortable when peace comes, but it will be boring. Since the ultimate goal of human society is happiness, we must also create a society of performing artists, to expect total happiness."

Miraculous Achievement #20

Grand Master Rhee was a State Guest of President Chen, Shui Bien of Taiwan from June 5-9, 2007.

Grand Master Rhee and his wife were invited to Taiwan as State Guests of President Chen, Shui Bien for five days, from June 5-9, 2007, to share his philosophy of TRUTOPIA. Grand Master Rhee gave speeches to several government agencies, universities, and business groups. He and Mrs. Rhee spent two-and-a-half-hours at a state dinner with the President on the first day and another hour-and-a-half at tea on the last day. Grand Master Rhee also gave a private Taekwondo demonstration for the President.

Their key interest was in a better relationship between the US and Taiwan. Grand Master Rhee always shared his Truth, Beauty, and Love (TBL) philosophy wherever he was invited to speak. Knowing that smoking and drinking are major problems for teenagers, Grand Master Rhee was bold enough to ask the host not to serve alcohol with their meals, and they cordially accepted his request.

Grand Master Rhee was invited by the government of Morocco to give a few speeches for Air Morocco, certain government agencies, and at universities. He was well received by the audiences and stayed in the country for five days. It was his first trip to the African continent, and he enjoyed it very much.

Grand Master Rhee must have done a good job in the country because he and Mrs. Rhee were asked to be guests of honor at a dinner party given by His Excellency Ambassador Aziz Mekouar of Morocco at his residence on May 5, 2008. Over 100 friends of the Ambassador and of Grand Master Rhee attended the dinner. Nancy Schultz, the wife of Congressman Richard Schultz, sang with a noted violinist, her friend David Fisher, presenting a beautiful show. Nancy used to be a member of Bob Hope's USO Show.

Grand Master Rhee's students Masters Francis Pineda, Amy Dudrow, and Shannon Wong performed Martial Ballet to the National Anthems of Morocco, America and Korea, and Grand Master Rhee played his harmonica. Guests were delighted to see their good friends Senator & Mrs. George Allen, Rep. Duncan Hunter, Toby Roth, Jack Kingston, Ben Chandler, Joe Wilson, and James and Mrs. Symington, Korean Ambassador, His Excellency Lee, Tae Sik, Georgetown Dean of International Studies and former Assistant Secretary of State, Robert Gallucci, and many others. The evening was very pleasant and most enjoyable. Grand Master Rhee was grateful to His Excellency, the Moroccan Ambassador, and Mrs. Aziz Mekouar.

2007. 6. 5 中華民國（台灣）總統府
Office of the President of the Republic of China (Taiwan)

2007. 6. 5 中華民國（台灣）總統府
Office of the President of the Republic of China (Taiwan)

Grand Master Rhee demonstrating flexibility and board breaking for
President Chen, Shui Bien after a state dinner.

Miraculous Achievement #21

Grand Master Rhee conducted the OVAL Conference for student leaders from Beijing, Seoul, and Tokyo Universities from February 9-13, 2009.

OVAL stands for Our Vision for Asian Leadership and consists of student leaders of the elite universities in Seoul, Beijing, and Tokyo. The world's major problem is the lack of trust among nations. In order to prepare for the future, we must train our youth for better mutual understanding when someday these student leaders become national leaders. OVAL can also be for American and African youth, not only Asian, and eventually will become a global student leaders conference.

Previously, on March 4, 2002 in Seoul, the Grand Master had formed the 10021 Club International Leadership Union with the blessings of 700 VIPs who attended the official Club formation. 10021 stands for both "100 Years of Wisdom in a Body 21 Years Young" as well as "TRUTOPIA will be accomplished by the end of the 21st Century." The 10021 Club International conducted a five-day conference for OVAL from February 9-13, 2009, in Jeju Island. About 80 elite university students from Tokyo, Beijing, and Seoul discussed various matters of international concern.

Grand Master Rhee's personal contribution to this conference was providing elite university student leaders with opportunities to become acquainted with others of their age. When they become the leaders of their countries and have summits 30 or 40 years later, they will not be strangers but old friends. This will make the future summits very productive meetings. The current plan is to create another OVAL, which will stand for Our Vision for American Leadership, to include Mexico, Canada, and America.

The 10021 Club International did not organize OVAL initially. It was organized by a think-tank in Japan in 2003. Then OVAL was left to the students themselves, and understanding its mission of international leadership, they approached the 10021 Club International for help. The students loved this first event in conjunction with the 10021 Club because its philosophy is exactly what OVAL needs. The students agreed, the best OVAL conference they ever attended was the one on Jeju Island in February 2009.

Now we can see Grand Master Jhoon Rhee to be truly a man of many miracles, a world-historical individual whose visions for the future, however mocked at first, have come true over the years for the good of all people around the globe. Today, his greatest and most profound vision is of the miracle of TRUTOPIA.

Grand Master Rhee's greatest miraculous achievement will be when he sees his vision of TRUTOPIA come true by the end of the 21st century.

TRUTOPIA

By
Jhoon Rhee
Taekwondo Grand Master

Acknowledgements

I am thankful to Korea, the birthplace of Taekwondo, for providing me with a profession through which I have grown, thrived, and ultimately formed the basis for TRUTOPIA.

I am thankful to the American Founding Fathers and Civil Rights Leaders, whose inspiring struggles for freedom have provided me with the foundation for building a TRUTOPIA society "where everyone is happy with every breath of life."

I am thankful to the Honorable Mikhail Gorbachev for opening up the former Soviet Union to the freedoms that humanity has fought for throughout history. Gorbachev, in my personal opinion, is one of the greatest men of the 20th Century for having stopped the three-quarter-century-old Cold War.

I am thankful to my first wife Hansoon, who died of cancer after 29 years of marriage, and my current wife Theresa, my grandparents, parents, brothers and sisters, relatives, mentors, teachers, students, fans and supporters around the world. Without your love, help, patience, and open minds, I would not have achieved what I have in martial arts as well as in life.

I am thankful to Mr. Hogap Kang, Chairman and CEO of Shinyoung Co. Ltd., whose support of this project has been generous and deeply appreciated.

I am thankful to two of my editors, Jim Werner and Herb Borkland, and Mrs. Sooki Moon and Lisa Werner, my book's designers.

I am thankful to the Creator, who enlightened me by a new realization of what is the True Will of God. It is important to believe in God, but it is more important to know the Will of God and work to realize it. What, then, is the Will of God?

1. For Jews, Christians, and Muslims, it is to create the Kingdom of God "on Earth as it is in Heaven."

2. For Buddhists, it is to make Paradise on Earth.

3. For all others, it is to bring about a healthy, wealthy and happy human society.

My other important new realization is understanding that people are waiting for God to work His Will, while God is waiting for us to be the ones who bring about His Will. All that will come about from this stand-off is an eternity of waiting.

We the people must complete the work of creation. God has done everything He can for us. The tiny portion that remains to be accomplished is for us to live by nothing but Truth, Beauty, and Love, to become saints for each other.

Table of Contents

Preface

This is a story of the life that has led to my beliefs, and the beliefs that have led to the life I have lived. As I approach the publication of this important book, TRUTOPIA, I think back to the early 1960s. I had just opened my first professional Jhoon Rhee Taekwondo School in Washington, DC on June 28, 1962. Within five years, I was able to expand my operations to five schools. At each of the monthly Taekwondo promotional tests for all these schools, I gave motivational speeches.

As the number of schools expanded, I was called upon to speak and demonstrate Taekwondo almost every week. This gave me the perfect opportunity to practice speaking publicly. My emphasis in my speeches has always been on positive thinking. My favorite quote used to be: "We can achieve as far as our thoughts can reach." Then, I realized that I was not living up to what I had been preaching. One day, my inner voice told me: "Jhoon, you have been saying that you can achieve as far as your thoughts can reach. So, why don't you seek out the biggest thought anyone can conceive?"

I was embarrassed, feeling I was merely a big talker, not a doer. The biggest goal I could imagine would be to own the entire world. With a smile, however, I knew this would cause me many headaches. So I decided that the biggest goal without headaches would be to help all people to be "happy with every breath of life." It reminded me of one of my favorite quotes from George Bernard Shaw:

"Some men see things as they are and say, why? I dream things that never were and say, why not?"

Utopia is a name coined by Sir Thomas More in 1516 to describe an ideal community on a fictional island in the Atlantic Ocean—an imaginary perfect society that is impossible to achieve.

Karl Marx conceived of his own utopian society, communism, which proved to be impossible to actualize because of the existence of greed. In contrast, a moral utopia would automatically bring about an economic, political, and social utopia. If Karl Marx had considered that deceptive human nature could be the problem to realizing communism, he would have warned future executors of communism, such as Lenin or Stalin, to educate people to be honest, first. This would then have resulted in the establishment of something I call "Happyism" or "Free Common Possessionism." I renamed it TRUTOPIA in 2007.

I am a firm believer that we can achieve as far as our brains can conceive. The airplane, light bulb, telephone, television, computer, internet, and many other things exist today because someone believed in them many years ago.

Thomas Moore's conception of Utopia can become a reality only by first beginning with an absolutely honest human conscience. With the perfect human conscience as our starting point, we can educate the six billion humans to perfect their imperfect consciences. This, then, is my concept of a TRUTOPIA: a solid, realistic world rather than one of wishful thinking. Something becomes reality only when an individual is dedicated to making it happen. I am committing myself to making TRUTOPIA a reality within the 21st Century.

I believe that people can achieve as far as their thoughts can reach. My feeling is that one day hydrogen will be the only source of clean, safe, powerful and renewable energy. Because of its abundance in water, hydrogen energy could be free to all. Since this idea has already been achieved, it will be a reality within a decade or two. When all six billion people have access to free energy, there will be no need to cheat and this world will become a TRUTOPIA sooner than we think.

In my quest to establish TRUTOPIA, I have looked for answers to such persistent questions as:

"Who am I?"
"Why am I living?"
"What are my values?"
"How do we define what is good and what is evil?"

Using conscientious reasoning for more than 45 years of my life, I have developed some interesting insights into these age-old human questions. The purpose of learning any new information is to be able to perform some action correctly. Ideas do not make things happen, but the proper execution of ideas always does.

The mind has a body, of course, but the body has a mind of its own. So we must repeat all the good ideas in the brain through action, again and again, until they are registered in the "brains" of all our muscle cells. When ideas have registered in the muscle-cell brains, they are called "habits" and "skills." Actions repeated with good ideas develop into good habits. Likewise, we must take action based on Truth, Beauty, and Love – TBL. By Practicing TBL in our daily lives we will develop good habits and life skills.

For a brick wall to stand, it needs cement; to put two pieces of paper together, we need glue; for people to stick together, there must be trust that works like glue. Trust comes from us daily leading by example.

"A picture is worth 1,000 words; an action is worth 1,000 pictures." *Jhoon Rhee*

Effective communication is the intelligent management of human emotion. Good leaders must learn how to communicate effectively by articulating positive words such as truth, beauty, love, and happiness. These words must flow, not just from their lips, but also out of the deepest heart of their life experiences. Then, they will make people want to march upon the road they have paved with spoken words.

Respect and trust are the two most important qualities of an effective leader. These qualities can be earned only through leading by example. One of the most beautiful aspects of America is her valuing of diversity. As former US Deputy Attorney General and now Georgetown University Law Professor Viet Dinh noted, "Diversity is not a problem; it is not an ideology. It simply is a demographic fact of life that defines us as universal people."

A rainbow is created by harmonizing a million diverse shades of different colors. A rainbow is a signpost from nature, demonstrating how we can live in a beautiful human society by harmonizing all differences of creed, race, religion, and national origin. Our world must follow America's example in this regard. I was proud to notice that America was the one of very few countries represented by several different races at the Olympic Games. I hope one day each nation will honor diversity as America has learned to do.

I hope all readers of this book will come to the same new realizations as have I. I may seem too idealistic to many of the 6 billion people in the world today, but as we witness from the recent election of President Barack Obama, the world is indeed advancing closer towards building TRUTOPIA.

After watching President Obama's Inauguration, I was overwhelmed by the change taking place in America. It was only 40 years ago, in the late 1960s, when I was a young student studying civil engineering at the University of Texas, that I witnessed African Americans denied their civil rights. On one occasion, I even saw an African American physically dragged out of a restroom by the police.

I am proud of how America is making dramatic progress toward providing what Thomas Jefferson described as "Life, liberty, and the pursuit of happiness" for all Americans. The scene of President Obama's inauguration was audacious. My intrepid hope is that someday my four-decade dream of TRUTOPIA will help to bring about an even grander panoramic view of people of every race, nation, and creed living together as brothers and sisters of one happy global family.

The universal purpose of life is Happiness. There are many religions to help people achieve Happiness; yet, none are succeeding. Fortunately, every religion teaches the universal human values of Truth, Beauty, and Love; yet, their followers have been fighting one another since the beginning of human history. What is the reason?

If we know the reason and eliminate it, there will be peace on earth. Most religions are selfishly motivated to teach the only way to true Happiness is through THEIR RELIGION. If every religion would teach to respect and honor universal ideas that are common to all religions, we would soon unite around the logical universal values, not around any religious identity.

There is nothing more divine in heaven and earth than human reason, because God's reason and people's reason must be common in order for God to understand our prayers. If all religions teach their followers the universal values, without identifying themselves, we will see TRUTOPIA on earth sooner than we think, once and for all.

The publication of TRUTOPIA has been a dream gestated for nearly five decades, ever since my first Taekwondo class in the US Congress gym on May 6, 1965. Not too long before, I had been a house boy for American soldiers. Now I felt as if God had appointed me the Taekwondo teacher for Congress. I had another experience just as unique, prior to this honor, when I first arrived in America at the San Francisco Airport on June 1, 1956. "What a contrast!" I marveled to myself. Yesterday I was in post-war Korea, living in hell; suddenly, today I found myself in a paradise.

I arrived here determined to find out the root strength of the United States. In my sincere research, I was inspired by the American Founding Fathers' mission statement placing upon America the responsibility to serve as the vanguard nation for a moral and political emancipation of all mankind. And what has America done for the world to fulfill her mission statement? Jesus taught, "There is no greater love than giving your life for your friend."

However, what about giving your life for a stranger? After the Korean War broke out in 1950, 34,000 precious young American lives were sacrificed for the good of people they had never met.

When World War II ended, who helped two enemy nations, Japan and Germany, to become the most powerful countries economically in the Far East and Europe, respectively? And after the recent terrible earthquake in Haiti, which was the first nation to extend a big helping hand?

I was a small, weak, and uncoordinated boy in my early years. When I ran track, I always came in last or next to last among the other first-grade students. I was so timid when I was six that I got beaten up by a five year old girl. When I came to my mother to be comforted; she asked me what had happened. When I told her the story, she was so disappointed in me, she beat me even harder!

I had been depending on my mother for the solution to every problem I had. When I found out she wasn't going to be the answer to all my problems, I knew I had to build the strength to stand on my own two feet. From then on, I began to exercise – push-ups, sit-ups, and how to punch and kick. When I was 14 years old, I found a martial arts studio near my house in Seoul, Korea. I took the martial arts to my heart and decided to introduce martial arts in America someday.

Ten years later, that remote dream of mine, to go to the United States, became a reality when I came to America for a short military training program in 1956. And later I returned to America again for my college education in Texas in 1957.

I am forever grateful to Dr. and Mrs. Frosty Rich, who found my sponsors, Mr. and Mrs. Robert L. Bunting of San Marcos, Texas in 1956, making it possible for me to return to start my college education in 1957. As always, my ultimate goal in coming to the US was not only for my own education but to introduce Taekwondo, Korean culture's unique fighting art.

In retrospect, three of my life's most miraculous achievements led me to TRUTOPIA.

1. An uncoordinated, timid boy became "The Father of Modern Taekwondo in the Western Hemisphere."

2. My young life in a hell in Korea lasted until May 31, 1956, when, in just one day, I moved up to Paradise in the US, on June 1st.

3. A house boy for US soldiers in 1945 came to be promoted to Taekwondo teacher for everyone from Muhammad Ali, the beloved boxing champion, to nearly 350 members of the United States Congress during the last 45 years, and millions of students around the world these past 54 years.

After thinking over this record of my life, I asked myself: "Why not promote today's insane state of global human society to TRUTOPIA?" – to God's original design of human society for all His children's happy lives.

Due to my absolute commitment to create TRUTOPIA, I have been living nothing but truth for the last 48 years. I believe I have been enlightened by a set of simple and logical answers to all the problems that are attacking this world. The Taekwondo philosophy, TRUTOPIA, has clarified the universal purpose of life, and from this purpose TRUTOPIA derives universal human values and creates clear definitions of good and evil.

Fortunately for us there is only one cause for millions of problems attacking this world today. This single cause is deceptive human nature when motivated, not by the human conscience, but by animal instincts. Therefore, the only job for us to concentrate on is to restore the contaminated human conscience through TRUTOPIA, the Taekwondo philosophy which I call Lead by Example Action Philosophy.

We must strive to achieve human perfection. I define human perfection as a person who never knowingly makes a mistake. If we all live with one simple habit – never do the things we know we shouldn't; and always do the things we know we should – we all will be humanly perfect. Here is my TRUTOPIA version of what James Madison wrote:

"If all men are angels, no government will be necessary."

Let us all commit ourselves to becoming humanly perfect, like angels, to make TRUTOPIA a reality as soon as possible. My vision of TRUTOPIA is so clear that I am compelled to commit to it until I graduate from the planet. If you believe that TRUTOPIA is indeed a worthy vision, please contact me, and let's work together for the generations to come.

Jhoon Rhee
http://www.JhoonRhee.com

"First 24 Years Of My Life In Korea" (1932-1956)

I was born into a humble family in Sanyangri, Asan, Korea on January 7, 1932. My father, Jin Hoon, and my mother, Kay Im Rhee, already had two daughters, Namgoo and Ahngoo, born in 1924 and 1928, respectively. When I was expected, my parents were very concerned because they desired a son. In the old days, almost 99% of Korean parents preferred to have boys over girls.

The reasons were very obvious. Throughout Korean history, the value of a woman was unfairly considered to be inferior to that of a man. Women were expected to serve men. I remember how my mother served her husband almost like a king in my childhood. You can see how welcomed a baby I was. I thank God that He made me a baby boy, otherwise I wouldn't be in Taekwondo today.

Most pregnant mothers in Korea have a "conception dream" called, in Korean, Taemong. Naturally, my mother had one too, when I was first conceived. She told me the story of her Taemong of me. "I was in a palace which was surrounded by a high and heavy castle wall, and I heard a roaring sound of a tiger, then I woke up," she said.

Years later, in 1962 and 1963, my Taekwondo activities were receiving newspaper, television, and radio coverage in the United States and Korea. By then my parents thought the Taemong dream was a very interesting coincidence.

When I was a little under eleven months old, my sister Nam was baby-sitting me and dropped me on a hard floor. My right thigh bone was broken at the midpoint between my knee and the hip. That same day my grandfather (Mr. Hong, Chong Ki, on my mother's side) died of an intestinal problem. My mother carried me to her father, who was about 5 miles away from where we lived. My mother told me that she had used her deceased father's hand to massage my broken thigh. In the old days, Koreans believed in such ideas. And it is true my broken thigh was miraculously and completely healed after only one visit to a doctor.

She told me she felt guilty that her concern for her son's broken thigh had taken precedence over mourning for her father. Her sense of sadness had been overshadowed by her love for me. This must be the mother's love, which children never quite appreciate. My parents never expected that I would someday be in such a physical profession, which would use that once broken thigh to jump and kick. Certainly, you cannot predict the future of a child by past experience.

My grandfather had four sons, Sunghoon, my father Jinhoon, Shihoon, and Manhoon, and one daughter, Soonwon. When I was five years old I was sent to our uncle Sunghoon's home for a year while his children were sent to my parents' home. This "exchange program" was created for children to build independent attitudes at an early age.

The psychology of this idea was that children do not depend on their aunt for every little thing as they do on their own mothers. During the early years of my life, I learned to respect parents and elders. My grandfather and uncle taught me a lot during the year I was with them. They taught me to be cheerfully obedient to parents and elders at home and to teachers in school. I was taught that my first duty each morning was to greet my grandfather and uncle with a deep kneel-down bow, saying, "Did you have a peaceful rest through the night, sir?"

I was taught to address Sir or Ma'am at the end of every phrase or sentence of my conversations with elders. I was taught to stand up when my grandfather, father, or uncle came into the room and to remain that way until I was told to sit. I was taught to be silent when an elder spoke and to answer briefly, only when I was asked. My grandfather was a scholar with a doctor's degree in Confucian Literature from Sung Kyun Kwan University, which presently is located in Seoul, Korea.

He was a man of high character and wisdom, with a loving personality. I loved him very much and miss him a lot. He lived a long life of 92 years, which is quite unusual considering the primitive medical facilities of Korea at that time. I attribute his long, healthy life to his morning stretching exercises, which he practiced religiously for about 30 minutes every day. I designed my "Jhoon Rhee Daily Dozen" (12 daily stretching exercises of the Jhoon Rhee Taekwondo Curriculum) based on my memories of watching his exercises and also on certain Yoga exercises. I was enrolled in Gul Bang, meaning "Room for Words," which is equivalent to a kindergarten in America. My grandfather gave me a book to study in Gul Bang. One day, I lost the book by carelessly leaving it in the school playground. When I came home, my grandfather asked me to bring my book to read, to see how much I had learned. I told him I had loaned the book to my friend. To my surprise, he took the book out and showed it to me. You can imagine how scared I was to be caught in my first lie.

My grandfather said I had to be disciplined for two reasons. First, for being careless with my book, and second, for the big lie I had just told. My five-year-old brain knew that I was wrong, so I took his spanking without any ill-feeling against him. He said softly, "My child, don't you know that whenever you lie, cheat, or steal, God is watching; and whenever you do good, you are also being watched? Do you understand, my child?" I answered, "Yes, Sir." What he said made one of the greatest impressions on me of anything in my life. I believe it was the most important moment of my life in building my character.

One day, a year later, my grandfather called me into his room and asked me, "Do you miss your mom, my child?" I answered, "Yes, sir." With his smiling face, he said, "Your mom is coming tomorrow to take you back home, so that you can begin your grammar school there." My face lit up with such joy, and I screamed, "Really, sir?"

That night I couldn't sleep because I was anticipating seeing my mom, from whom I had been separated for a whole year. Although it was only 50 miles between my home and grandfather's, it took a day or two, due to the traffic conditions of that time. Today, it takes only a little over an hour. What a change in our world within only 50 years!

My grandfather got up around six o'clock every morning, and I usually slept until eight. But, on the morning of my mother's arrival, I woke up before five, and I had to wait for over an hour before my morning greeting to my grandfather. I was too happy to sleep. I was so excited to see my mom that I tried to meet her along the road. She was arriving by train at Shin-Chang, a small village with a train station about five miles from my grandfather's house.

A little after five o'clock in the afternoon, I saw my mom approaching, about 300 feet away. I ran toward her as fast as I could. When I reached her, I was about to dash into her arms, but she seemed indifferent and not ready to take me. I was so embarrassed, when I realized that she was not my mom, I cried. About ten minutes later, another lady was approaching me, but this time I was very careful not to make the same mistake. This time, she was running, so I was pretty sure that she was my mom; still, I felt somewhat cautious. When I ran into her arms, I cried, and so did she, but I could tell she was trying to hide her tears from me.

I carried her bag all the way to my grandfather's house. It was the happiest moment of my life. A few days later, we returned home to Suwon, and I was enrolled in Shinpoong Grammar School, where I spent the next six years, until I was eleven. My father was employed as a clerk of a small company. One day when I was in second grade, I visited my father on the way home from school. He gave me two pennies for no reason. I asked him, "What do you want me to buy, sir?" He replied, "Buy candy for yourself." I could not believe my father, whom I feared, gave me money to buy candy.

I was happily surprised and grateful because I had never experienced a feeling of love from my father until that day. I knew he was my important and precious father, but I was never sure that he loved me. I did not spend the pennies on candy but instead brought home a few clams for my daddy's favorite clam soup. My mom was wondering how I got those clams, so I told her the story. She was touched by her little son's sweet thought. I was told that I was almost always a good and obedient boy to my parents and teachers – which may have been because I was afraid not to.

One day, when I was six years old, I came home crying for a mother's comfort. My mother asked me why I was crying. I told her that I had been slapped by Soonduck, a five-year old girl who used to be one of our neighbors. Although I was one year older, she was a tough little girl. My mother slapped me, too, and so hard, I didn't know where I was for a moment. She was really upset with her son for getting slapped by a girl who was a year younger.

That moment, I decided to do something with myself, to stand on my own two feet. In other words, I had to be strong and confident about myself, to take care of myself. There were no Taekwondo studios in my hometown of Suwon back then; the only thing I could think of doing was weight-lifting. So I lifted weights for a few years, until I was thirteen, when I moved to Seoul, where I began my middle school education.

After I graduated from grammar school in 1943, I was sent to my Uncle Manhoon's in Seoul, Korea. There I was enrolled at Dong Sung High School. In our school system, we had two vacations a year, one in summer and the other in winter, each a month long. I visited my grandfather during all my summer and winter vacations until I graduated from high school.

It was during the summer vacation, when I first heard that Korea was liberated from Japanese occupation on August 15, 1945. I vividly remember that I was so excited over the news, I screamed, "WE ARE FREE!" I also remember my cousins gave me funny looks which made me feel stupid about being so excited. I was not old enough yet to really understand the significance of the National Liberation, but I did have some idea that it was important for the Korean people.

In September, I returned home to Suwon, where I found our family had moved to a bigger house. My father had purchased it from a Japanese family who had to leave Korea. Two violins came with the house. At that time, owning a violin was, for me, beyond my imagination. I wanted to learn how to play. I began to practice them, but there was no formality in my practice. I created my own note for each of the four strings, and learned a few Korean folk songs to play by ear. I enjoyed playing the violin very much.

In 1946, there was an annual school talent show where I had the first opportunity to play my violin and harmonica before an audience. The school principal was Dr. Chang, Myun, who later became the first Korean Ambassador to the United States under Sigman Rhee (not a relative of mine) and later the Prime Minister of Korea, when President Sigman Rhee was overthrown by an unorganized uprising of students on April 19, 1960.

I did not play fancy classical songs like "Gold and Silver" or "Silver Wedding." Instead, I played a few Korean folk songs like Torajee and Yangsando, which we usually heard from the local herb medicine salesman trying to attract street-side customers. The next morning, I had a new nick name: "Yakjangsa," which means "quack medicine salesman." Anyway, I did have the honor of shaking hands with the principal, Dr. Chang, Myun.

I had always been the smallest kid in my classes until I was in seventh grade. There I found a boy who was even smaller than I was. He really made me feel good and became a good friend. You may never believe that I was a very uncoordinated boy. Whenever we had a race, I always finished either last or second to last. And I often came home crying because I could not take care of myself against bullies. I used to be embarrassed and frustrated. Those bullies motivated me to learn Taekwondo. That is how my interest in Taekwondo training began.

It was in September 1947, when I first enrolled myself in Chung Do Kwan to learn Tang Soo Do, now called Taekwondo. Chung Do Kwan was founded by Grand Master Won Kook Lee. I gave my heart to Taekwondo training, to be the best someday. In the old times, Taekwondo was not as popular as it is today, and to my conservative father, it was not much better than street fighting. So, for the first three months, I did not inform my father that I had started taking Taekwondo lessons. Three months later, my father came to Seoul to visit us and found out that I was taking Taekwondo. My uncle was able to persuade him to give his approval, which I had to have.

When Korea was liberated on August 15, 1945, American movies flooded into the country. It was illegal for middle or high school students to attend any movie theater at that time. One day a friend of mine and I went to a theater illegally anyway. I had never seen so many beautiful girls in my life. That evening, I set as my goal that someday I would marry one of those beautiful American blondes.

But I did not know how I was going to find a blonde in Korea. I knew that the only way to achieve my goal was to find a way to go to America. I also had to think about supporting my future family and myself in the US I thought that I would introduce Taekwondo to the United States. The opportunity did not come for a long, long time, but I prepared myself to be ready as soon as an opportunity arose.

With this in mind, I began to study English harder than any other subject. In the ninth grade, I had a very good English teacher, Mr. Kwang Kim. One day, Mr. Kim picked me to read and translate a paragraph from our English text book. I was very lucky that I prepared myself well for that day and did a very good job. He complimented me so much in front of all my classmates, I was somewhat embarrassed but quite happy and very encouraged. From that point on, I was motivated to study even harder. From ninth grade through the 12th grade, English was the best of all my subjects.

For two years, only a few close friends knew that I was taking Taekwondo. One day in the eleventh grade, a popular bully snatched the pencil out of my hand without saying anything. I politely asked him to give the pencil back. All he said was, "Shut up." I told him I would see him after school. He accepted the challenge.

After classes, we both went to the vineyard behind the school where no one could see us. I was a brown belt then, and for the first time in my life, I was about to test my fighting ability against one of the most notorious bullies in school. I knew if I passed this test, I was going to be one of the most confident boys in the whole school. I was very nervous, but it was too late to worry about it. I did my best to win the fight.

He swung at me first, and I punched him in the left eye and kicked him in the throat. He immediately gave up the fight saying: "You got me." I couldn't believe what I had just done by beating one of the toughest guys in the whole school! The next day, the bully showed up with a big black eye, and he had to tell his friends the story of how it happened. From that moment on, I was treated better and given more respect by my classmates. I felt very good. I enjoyed going to school a lot more. I personally gained my peace through strength.

In early June 1950, after my graduation from high school, I was accepted at the Dong Kook University. A few days later, we had a freshmen class election for student government. Somehow I was elected vice president of the freshmen class. One of my duties was to collect the monthly tram ticket coupon fees from all freshmen students at the University. I collected the money, with an estimated value today of about $500, which I had to carry with me until all the collections were completed.

Then the Korean War broke out on June 25, 1950. It was the biggest surprise to every Korean. My younger brother Jungoo (nine years old) and I (18 years old) fled toward the South. We arrived at our grandfather's around the fourth of July. A few days later, North Korean Communist troops passed us in Asan, where my grandfather used to reside. We stayed there for a month. We missed our mother, who was still staying at our home alone in Suwon. My nine year old brother Jungoo (Sam) and I walked 50 miles to our home in Suwon to see our mother. It took us three days to complete the trip. When we arrived home, the house was empty. We were worried about our mother. Three hours later our mother came home with a sack full of acorns for her daily meal.

I was 19 years of age, the perfect age to be drafted by the North Korean military. So I was hiding for a month in the underground cell where we stored our kimchi so it would not spoil in summer, until US soldiers reoccupied Suwon after the successful Inchon landing operation by the great General Douglas MacArthur on September 15, 1950. On January 4, 1951, North Korea recaptured Seoul with the help of the Chinese army. At that time I was working as a dishwasher in one of the US Air Force base's K-13 kitchens in Suwon.

I was fortunate to be included among a few Korean personnel to be evacuated by the US Air Force. Up to this point, I was a fair reader of English; however, using English in conversations was new to me. I needed to learn conversational English very quickly to perform my job successfully.

I left my mother, brother, and sister behind for Chinhae. Naturally, I was very uneasy by myself because my family could not go with me. I was away from home for two months, until early February 1951. I came home when the UN forces pushed the Communist Chinese forces close to the 38th parallel. When I got home, I found that half of my house was destroyed by a US air attack when the enemy force was occupying my hometown. Fortunately, none of my family members were injured. I looked for a new job again, but it was not easy finding one so far from the front line. However, I heard that there were plenty of jobs at the front line for those who had some knowledge of English.

I decided to take a chance on a new job with any US Force. The only way to travel near the front line was to hitchhike on the highways. First, I went to a US Army Post near my home in Suwon and asked for a ride to any place near the front line. An hour later, a jeep arrived driven by a lieutenant in a combat helmet. The guard asked the officer, "Sir, this young man is looking for a job. Could you use him or give him a ride near the front line?" He asked me, "Can you speak English?" I replied, "Yes, sir." "Come on in," he said. I quickly responded, and we had a long ride together. He wanted me to work as his house boy, and I accepted happily.

A week later, I was promoted to an interpreter for the US 25th Infantry Division Military Police Company. Generally, Korean laborers were not treated nicely by American soldiers, but I didn't have any problems with it because, whenever I got a new job, I always let everyone know that I was a Black Belt in Taekwondo. I loved the officers for whom I worked, but I didn't like the weather too much. My boss appreciated what I was doing and gave me a Longines, which was the first wristwatch I ever owned in my life.

It was too cold for me to stay any longer, so I resigned from the Post in early April 1951. I came to Seoul, the Capital of South Korea, where I had attended high school for six years. By this time, I had over one year of experience as an English interpreter and had gained confidence in myself. It was a tough life and challenging for a 20-year-old filled with a young spirit. Without an appointment, I visited the British Army Food Supply Company situated at the Seoul Railway Station.

Again I got a job as an interpreter. There I had to supervise over 100 laborers, many of who were tough and nasty. My Taekwondo came in handy again. About a week later, I planned a one-man Taekwondo demonstration at lunchtime for all the British officers, soldiers, and laborers. I must have made some impression on everyone because everyone became very friendly with me. It made my job easier and more enjoyable. I held that job until December 1951, when I was drafted by the Korean Army.

I was sent to the Nonsan Army Basic Training Camp for a 12-week training program. It was a hellish life because of all I had to go through during the training. Working for the American and British forces was a paradise compared to the camp. We were always hungry, cold, tired, and we received lots of physical punishment from mean sergeants. It is impossible to describe the hardship we had to go through.

It was in April 1952 when I was transferred to Chulwon, where the 101st Artillery battalion was newly formed near the front line. It was very cold, and we lived in a field tent without heat, and with only one blanket per person. Our meal consisted of three spoons of rice and a couple sips of salt water, which was supposed to be soup. We were allowed to sleep no more than three or four hours a day. I did not have to go to the bathroom more than twice a month, at the most, because the commanding officer sold three-fourths of our food supply on the black market to fill his own pocket.

I thought my life during the 12 week training was hell. I was wrong. It was heaven compared to my new life in the 101st Battalion. I wanted to die so many times. But I just didn't have the guts to do so. If the commander had been taught basic human ethics, would his conscience have allowed him to commit such crimes? During the Korean War, the corruption of government and military officers was a very serious problem.

One day I heard an announcement about Officers Cadet School recruiting. At that time, everybody knew that 70 percent of the newly commissioned officers were killed in action. That was the reason I had never applied to be an officer. Now I did not care. All I cared about was getting out of the 101st Battalion. I applied and easily passed the exam. I was sent to the Officers Cadet School in Kwangjoo, Korea. It was hard training, but I was fed three meals a day and had six hours of sleep each night in a nice, warm room. I felt like a new man.

However, I was concerned about my life after I graduated from the Officers Cadet School. I knew I had only a 30 percent chance of surviving for more than a few months. I was not sure whether I had made the right decision. I wrote my parents a letter saying that I had met a general who would help me stay at the Officers Cadet School as a Taekwondo instructor so that I would not be sent to the combat zone upon my graduation. It was a white lie told to comfort them.

Just a few weeks prior to graduation, the Truce was signed on July 27, 1953. I just could not believe that I was not going to die. The 250 young men of our graduating class were the happiest men in the world. It felt like getting a presidential pardon from capital punishment. My dead hope of promoting Taekwondo in the United States was alive again.

After my graduation, I applied to receive army aviation training. Later, I changed to weather and aircraft maintenance training. When I completed my training, I was assigned to stay at the Aviation School to teach weather and aircraft maintenance to pilot students. I taught for two and a half years.

One day I read an announcement to apply for an aircraft maintenance training program in the US I could hardly believe my luck. I was determined not to miss this opportunity. English was the most important subject, and there were not too many officers who could beat me in English. So I was quite confident that I had a good chance to make it. Among over 50 applicants, only three officers would be selected. Later I learned that I passed with the highest grade. Upon completion of a three month English language training program, I was scheduled to leave for Gary Air Force Base in San Marcos, Texas.

The day came on June 1, 1956. I just couldn't believe that my dream was coming true. It was my first experience of flying in a plane, to come to the United States. When I was seated on the plane, I even pinched my own cheek to make sure that this was not a dream. It was a long flight from Seoul to America. I first landed at the San Francisco International Airport, where I saw a flood of automobiles for the first time.

As a Korean soldier, I was used to seeing only green military vehicles; the automobiles – like everything else around me – were so impressive. "What a contrast! I was in a hell yesterday and now I am in a paradise the next day." During that day, I was given an opportunity to see the city of San Francisco. I could hardly believe the magnificent skyscrapers, colorful neon street signs, beautiful women drivers, and a Coke machine which was able to calculate and give me correct change. I felt I was in a dream world. It was not until the next day that I became impressed by the integrity of the American people in 1956.

I was sent to Austin, Texas by plane and eventually to the city's Greyhound Bus Terminal. There I waited three hours for a bus to take me to my final destination, Gary Air Force Base in San Marcos, Texas. About 10 minutes after the bus departed, I recalled I had forgotten to bring a bag which I had left on a waiting room bench at the terminal. It was too late to return to the bus station that evening so I took a bus back first thing the next morning. When I arrived at the bus station to look for what I left behind, I was very surprised. My bag stood still waiting in the very same spot I had left it. I couldn't believe what I had just experienced.

A few days later, my training program began without too many difficulties. There were about 20 students in the class, all Americans except for me. I was the shortest again and the only officer in the class. The courses I had to take were the ones I had already taken in Korea, so it was a perfect chance to study my English. A week later, on a Sunday morning, I visited the First Methodist Church in San Marcos, Texas. I put on my army uniform to get more attention from people. Sure enough, everyone started paying so much attention to me, as though I were a strange animal. Later I found out that many of them had never seen an Asian in person.

A few minutes prior to the church service, the Pastor came over to me, introduced himself, and asked me about myself. During the service, to my surprise, I was introduced to the whole congregation as if I were a V.I.P. "We have a special guest visiting us this morning: Lieutenant Jhoon Rhee, an army officer from Korea, who will be stationed at Gary Air Force Base for the next six months. Lieutenant Jhoon Rhee, would you please come forward." I approached the front, and he said, "Let's all welcome him to San Marcos." I was made to feel so welcome that I was even more determined to return to America as soon as possible.

I felt very comfortable in this totally unfamiliar place. I thought that it wouldn't be too difficult to find a friend who would sponsor me for my return to America, to realize my age-old dream. The only way I could return to America was to enroll in a college. I knew that I needed my general education in America, even though my goal was to teach Taekwondo.

After the service was over, among the many who came by to talk to me was a young couple, Rev. Frosty Rich and his beautiful wife, Betsy. They invited me to visit the Wesley Foundation on the campus of Southwest Texas State Teachers College in San Marcos, Texas. Frosty was in charge of the Wesley Foundation, where I met many new friends.

After that, I became a regular attendant of the Church and the Foundation. The most important mission I had to accomplish for myself during the next six months was to find a friend who would sponsor me for my return to America. I talked to Frosty and many other friends, explaining how much I wanted to return to continue my education at the campus. I told them that I needed an American citizen who would sponsor me. It was not very easy to sponsor somebody because the sponsor would be responsible for that person's welfare during his education. Frosty and Betsy worked hard to help find a sponsor for me, but I didn't receive the blessing. There was only one more week left before I had to go back home.

On the last Sunday church service, I was filled with sadness, thinking that my dream was going to remain only a dream. The whole city knew that I was looking for a sponsor, but no one seemed to be interested in helping me. I thought that Americans were cold people, only because I did not know the responsibilities one had to bear to sponsor a foreign student. I thought any American could loan his name, and it was done.

In the middle of the church service, I heard the Pastor. "Among the congregation, anyone who is interested in helping our friend Lt. Jhoon Rhee continue his education in America, please come forward." And to my surprise, I heard, "I will!" from an elderly gentleman, Mr. Robert L. Bunting, a real estate broker. Mr. and Mrs. Bunting came to me and took my hand and walked me up to the Pastor. Then everyone sang a hymn, and the Pastor led a prayer for my speedy and safe return to America. Later, I found out that Frosty and a few other friends knew of Mr. Bunting's decision to sponsor my return. He knew what his obligations were, and he met all the requirements to sponsor me as a student.

My dream was suddenly revived again. I was introduced to the President of the Southwest Texas State College, Dr. and Mrs. John G. Flowers, who later became my foster parents. After the church services, Mr. and Mrs. Bunting prepared a luncheon for me at their home with a few close friends, including my best friends, Frosty and Betsy Rich. I just couldn't believe this was happening to me. It was the happiest moment of my life. I was ready to go back to Korea to serve one more year of my obligation to the Korean Army and then return to America as a college student. Within nine months, I had completed all the necessary papers and received an honorary discharge from the Korean Army.

I returned to San Marcos, Texas on November 21, 1957. While I was waiting for the beginning of the Spring semester, Frosty asked me if I would join him to attend a Methodist college students conference scheduled to be held in Lawrence, Kansas. During the four-day conference, I was inspired by a Chinese student guest speaker – not by the contents of his speech, but by his ability to speak such fluent English. From that moment on, my immediate goal was to be able to speak like him. Soon after we returned from the convention, I registered for my courses, beginning on February 3, 1958.

This was how my new life began in America.

Chapter I: Seven Qualities of a Champion

A. Martial Arts as Action Philosophy

When I first became a Taekwondo instructor, I claimed that my martial art is a philosophy which can be very instrumental in developing our youth through mental discipline and physical conditioning. However, I had a difficult time justifying to myself how punching and kicking could be a philosophy. In the early 1970s, I was writing a column for *Blackbelt* magazine. The editor called on me to write an article to justify Taekwondo as a philosophy. I felt I was in trouble because I did not know what to say. During three months of research, I was able to develop my article, "Seven Qualities of a Champion," which has gone on to become quite popular among martial artists of various other styles.

Psychologists say that logic may not always activate an emotion, but actions always do. The most effective way to create a desired mental state is by a physiological activity which parallels this desired state. In other words, our state of mind is caused, not only by thoughts, but also through physiologies such as spoken words, actions, and chosen body postures. When I ask my audience: "Please try to be sad," almost everyone lowers their heads and shoulders. If I ask: "Try to be excited," then, nearly everyone raises their heads and straightens their body postures.

Dr. Bernie Siegel is the author of a book called *Love, Medicine and Miracles*. He is a surgeon who has worked with cancer patients using psychological imaging. What is fascinating is how closely the mind and body are related. For instance, he tells how twelve cancer patients were all given a pill and told it was a chemotherapy pill. However, six of the patients were given only a placebo. Guess what happened? All twelve patients, including those only given placebos, had their hair fall out. In other words, because these people believed the pill would cause their hair to fall out, this was the message their minds gave to their bodies, and their bodies reacted to it. Isn't that amazing?

From these observations, I was reassured that martial arts can be "action philosophies" which can help change our children's behavior. The teaching essence of martial arts must be philosophy, for martial arts without philosophy is merely street fighting.

Now let us examine how physical qualities can enhance human qualities which can be applied to our daily living. In a champion of martial arts and of life, we find corresponding parallel qualities.

There are seven basic physical qualities that are developed through martial arts training. These physical qualities can be transformed into human qualities because the body and mind are as inseparable as heat and light in a flame. It is an important psychological discovery that a motion triggers an emotion as much as an emotion triggers a motion. In other words, we are happy when we sing; also we sing when we are happy. In order to become a true champion of life and in the martial arts, we must develop the following human qualities by making a habit of positive actions.

B. Seven Qualities Of a Champion

1. Power/Knowledge/Capital Power

One will never become a champion in martial arts without developing power—developing mental and physical strength. We all have the potential for genius, and everyone can become an expert in at least one field, through which we can serve others for mutual happiness. There are two kinds of knowledge: that of worldly matters and of mental matters. Knowledge of worldly matters enable us to do something for ourselves, first, and then we can share it with others. Knowledge of mental matters enables us to develop good character for better human relationships with others.

Complementing knowledge of the mind is knowledge of worldly matters, which show us the way to intellectual strength. As we generate our physical strength through development of our muscles by daily exercise, we must also develop mental strength through development of our mental muscles in daily mental exercise—positive thinking, memorization, analysis, creativity, and problem solving.

A healthy body provides only for physical comfort but not for peace of mind or happiness. Honesty may bring peace of mind but not necessarily happiness, the ultimate purpose of life. An honest person may not harm anyone but without knowledge or skill, he or she cannot contribute to society.

True happiness comes from being physically free to do the things the mind desires. Mental and physical strengths together can provide us with the means to actualize our desires. A person is a product of their upbringing and education, with a seemingly limitless inborn capacity to learn if only one understands how to unlock his or her full potential.

As our bodies grow, so do our minds. One of the main causes of unhappiness is the daily mistakes we make either knowingly (crimes) or unknowingly (accidents); either way, they do hurt us. Through education, the human race has done much to improve its economic standards. I believe that everyone is born a genius and has the potential to achieve success if one has the right attitude and the desire to succeed.

"A genius is made by one percent inspiration and 99 percent perspiration."
Thomas Edison

I am very happy that our profession, the martial arts, is recognized as one of the most beautiful arts by the general public, especially when its movements are synchronized with music. John Adams, early in his professional life, implied that the purpose of studying is to enhance arts for the ultimate fulfillment of human happiness. We, as martial arts champions, must develop our powers by strengthening the body, heart, and mind, in order to effectively and efficiently learn how to continually apply our craft. The late legendary UCLA basketball Coach John Wooden, age 98, said:

"When I am through learning, then I am through."

As long as we live, we should never stop learning. So, let us cultivate power by developing strength in the body, honesty in the heart, and knowledge in the mind. We can increase our knowledge in the mind through constant learning, by listening to our conscience and reason, and from accumulating our knowledge of worldly matters by paying close attention to our teachers and the world around us. With both inner and outer forms of knowledge, we will develop strength within ourselves and be able to positively influence those around us.

As we martial artists develop a daily habit of exercising our muscles, to become champions, we also must develop a daily learning habit in order to become human champions. Those who develop daily habits of exercising and of learning surely will realize financial success as well as the true confidence and pride necessary for a happy life.

2. Quickness/Alertness/Awareness

The word "Accu-punch" was coined while I trained Muhammad Ali for his title-defending match against British champion Richard Dunn in Munich, Germany in 1976. I defined "Accu-punch" as a punch executed at the moment I decided to punch—a punch of the body and mind in synchronization. There should be no time gap between the decision and execution of a punch. This will not only eliminate telegraphed motion, but also increase acceleration and enormously increase power. I have been applying this principle in my daily life—"Never procrastinate."

When I conduct my martial arts seminars, I enjoy doing a punching demonstration with the help of two or three volunteers from the audience. I ask them to block a punch aimed at their faces. No one has ever been able to block this punch, although once by luck a gentleman did it in Hawaii. The truth is it is almost impossible to block, not only because my punch is fast, but also because I understand the psychological principle of "Accu-punch." This principle is to strike at the same instant the decision to punch is made.

When you see a red light while driving, you cannot step on the brake pedal at the same moment the light changes. It takes time to communicate—your eyes tell the brain, and your brain tells your foot to step on the brake. The length of time required to react is called "human reaction time." This lag is the reason why, when designing traffic lights, how long the yellow light lasts is determined by the speed limit and the width of each intersection. To be a champion in life, we must not only be able to physically react quickly, we must also develop the ability to think quickly when meeting challenges and solving problems in daily life.

Obviously, it is a very important principle for all fighters to punch without being blocked. The name of the game in a fight is to hit the enemy before he can hit you. Staying one step ahead of your opponent is the key to success. We may have no control over the techniques our opponents throw at us, but what is within our control is how we counterattack or initiate an offensive tactic.

By the same token, we have no control over our daily challenges; however, we do control how we prepare in advance and react to each incident. It is our attitude that determines the outcome of everything in our daily lives. Just as you will miss most targets without a habit of responding quickly, those who make a habit of procrastinating will not succeed in life because they are thieves of their own time.

So, let us develop a habit of thinking fast and staying one step ahead of the competition by always being prepared in daily life, just as we develop speed to stay ahead of an opponent in order to become a champion in martial arts. Remember, we should never procrastinate, for procrastinators are thieves of their own time.

3. Timing/ Punctuality/ On Time Delivery

In order to become a martial arts champion, one must develop near-perfect timing. Developing speed and power is not enough to become a champion. Being the quickest and strongest does not necessarily equate with success, unless that individual learns to act at the appropriate moments. During sparring, there is no time to think. Every move has to be made at the right moment in order for it to connect with the opponent. Through constant practice, we will be able to throw kicks and punches at the correct targets at the right moment.

By the same token, in order to become a champion in life, we must develop a habit of choosing the right moment and acting appropriately for success. This includes developing the daily habit of punctuality by honoring appointments made with our family, friends, peers, and other associates. As George Washington said,

"Discipline is the soul of an army."

The discipline to respect time is one way to develop self-respect, the first step toward respect for parents, teachers, and peers. There are many who are capable, yet fail in life due to the lack of discipline in their proper use of time. We are limited by time and space and must respect both of these by being punctual. With the habit of being punctual, we develop a good reputation and create credibility—qualities which are the basis for success in life. The expression, "To succeed, one must be at the right place at the right time," sums up the importance of timing in becoming a champion in life.

In my senior year at the University of Texas, one of my teachers said, "When you get your job, develop a habit of being at your office five minutes before work starts in the morning, and leaving your office five minutes after closing time; your boss sure will love you for that, and you will be the one to be promoted when the next vacant position is open."

So, let us develop punctuality in daily life, just as we develop a sense of good timing to become a champion in martial arts.

4. Endurance/ Perseverance/ Persistence

In the martial arts, a champion must train to develop stamina—a form of cardiovascular and muscular endurance. The Jhoon Rhee Institute created the "double-counter," a beginner's sparring training program which is a method to develop a student's determination to win. This program creates the habit of delivering a second or third counter when our attacks are blocked and counterattacked. Frequently, we do not succeed on the first attempt to counter our opponent's attack, but we usually do on the second or third try.

Thomas Edison, the greatest inventor in modern history, spoke words of wisdom after failing so many times in his experiments to develop the carbon-impregnated filament used in the first incandescent light-bulb. After 5,000 experiments, a young journalist asked why he persisted in his experiments after all these failures. Edison replied:

"Young man, you don't understand how the world works. I have not failed at all. I have successfully identified 5,000 ways that do not work. This just puts me 5,000 ways closer to the way it will work."

Depending on the individual, a sense of persistence can change, not only the destiny of one person, but all of human history.

Marvin White, one of my brown belt students, was born with fetal thalidomide syndrome—having only one leg, two elbows and only one thumb on the left elbow. He used to come to watch classes at one of our Taekwondo studios in Stafford, Virginia, where his younger brother had become a student. One day Master Ken Carlson, the head instructor, told Marvin that if he wanted to, he too could learn martial arts. He did not believe Master Carlson at first, but Master Carlson's persistent attempts finally persuaded Marvin to give it a try.

A year later, Marvin could break two boards with his spinning 360 degree wheel kick, two boards and one cinder block with his elbow, and one board held up head-high using a jump front kick. After his demonstrations, he touched many hearts, including mine, by saying to his audience: "I am not 'Marvelous Marvin,' but I am Happy Marvin. If I can be happy, there is no reason why anyone cannot be happy."

Persistence is meeting challenges, but it also includes the ability to develop and maintain a consistent level of success. Establishing consistency can be manifested through the universal practice of maintaining perfect attendance—arriving on-time to work or school each and every day.

Perfect attendance is emblematic of this principle because it shows the ability of the individual to give priority to what is important—their job or school. In order to establish perfect attendance, these individuals must not get distracted by lesser priorities or put themselves at risk of getting sick. While momentary successes may be difficult to achieve, long-term goals such as perfect attendance can be done but require persistent effort.

For instance, Hall of Fame baseball player Cal Ripken, Jr. was an outstanding shortstop and third baseman. However, he is known as "Iron Man" because he consistently maintained a high level of performance and kept himself healthy for 2,632 consecutive games—a span of over 16 years!

So, let us develop a sense of persistence in daily life just as we develop a sense of endurance to become a champion in the martial arts.

5. Balance/ Rationality/ Stability

In order to become a martial arts champion, we must have a good sense of physical balance; when you lose your balance in a fight, you may lose the fight. When you are kicking with one leg, you have only one leg to balance your body. Through disciplined training one must develop this sense of balance to become a martial arts champion.

I have repeated the motto of "strength in the body, honesty in the heart, and knowledge in the mind" many times in my writings, because our goal is to make all children of the next generation able to meet the qualifications for true humanhood: strength, honesty, and knowledge—a humanly perfect character.

A person of wisdom and character who is without strength will not be able to function physically; a person of wisdom and strength without character will be dangerous; and a person of character and strength but without knowledge will not be in high demand by any society. Therefore, it is our duty to build balanced qualities of health, character, and wisdom starting from the earliest age possible, before children become contaminated by negative social environments.

To be a champion in the martial arts, one must develop proficiency in the ability to use both hands and both feet. It is not sufficient to develop a dominant or strong side for punching or kicking. This will not only limit the possibilities of the individual, it will also create a dependency which can be exploited if the dominant side becomes injured.

Furthermore, a martial arts champion must be expert in using both feet and hands—four weapons are certainly greater than only one or two! By this same token, a champion in life needs to successfully balance good health due to proper diet (eating moderate quantities of good-quality food), exercise and rest, and by enjoying hobbies, as well as enjoying successes in interpersonal relations and at work or school.

We all have to balance our checkbooks. In the business world, our financial statements must be balanced. Families work on balancing their budgets. Our government is run on a basis of checks and balances and must continuously strive to balance the national budget. Politicians of any nation must balance their power by balancing executive, legislative, and judiciary branches of government.

Let us develop a sense of balance by cultivating strength in the body, honesty in the heart, and knowledge in the mind, just as a martial artist must also develop a sense of physical balance by training both sides of the body and by standing on one leg at a time.

6. Flexibility/ Gentleness/ Adaptability

Flexibility is one of the most important physical qualities for martial artists, especially when attempting to execute high kicks. More importantly, good flexibility helps prevent muscle and ligament injuries and helps us maintain our physical youth. By the same token, an open mind is at the core of becoming a champion in life.

The nature of water is the best example of the kind of flexible character which all people should learn. (Isn't it interesting that our bodies happen to be mostly composed of water?) Water is shapeless, colorless, odorless, and tasteless. When it is poured in a round container, its shape becomes round; square in a square container. When you add red dye, it becomes red water; blue water with blue dye and yellow, black, and so on.

When we drink water, it becomes our blood, hormones, tears, and many other forms of liquid which the human body needs. Water becomes wine with grapes or some other fruits; when it is mixed with soap, it becomes soapy water that can clean up dirt. When water is mixed with sand and cement, it becomes buildings.

Rain water comes from high heaven yet always seeks the lowest places on earth, to wet all the dry land, to give life to the plant kingdom which in turn gives life to the animal kingdom, including all of humankind. Then, the water as vapor quietly disappears into heaven again without claiming any credit.

Most dogmatic religions have their own fixed shapes like hard and cold ice. They claim to be the only truth by denying the beliefs of other religions. Rigidly conforming our beliefs to any religion's dogma freezes our potential and confines it into that religion's prescribed block of ice. Instead, let us all strive to become like water – limitless in our potential.

Today, too many conflicts are caused by rigid, close-minded people who lack any understanding of others. We should always be open-minded and respect others. One of the major social problems is the differences in the beliefs among people who follow dogmatic religions. Many people are taught, "Unless you believe in my God, you will go to Hell." This is really a narrow-minded view and very offensive to other people. I know people believe in the freedom of religion, yet some still believe that those who do not believe their religion will be damned for eternity.

I tried to find out the reason why some religions glorify suicide to please God; I discovered the reason. Some religions have taught people to live and die to honor God ever since human history began. I am not sure this teaching is the will of God. If God's love is unconditional, the teaching has to be changed. I am sure that most parents with these religious beliefs must be living with constant worry that their children may commit suicide.

I envisioned that God is very sad when people kill themselves for Him, just as we the physical parents will be heartbroken if our children kill themselves to please their parents — us. We must understand God is not selfish as we are. Although people are selfish, no parents demand their children to live and die for them. If God's love is unconditional, I believe God must be telling us:

"Children, I did not create you for My own glory at all; I created you for your own happy living. Don't worry about Me at all; just enjoy your life by loving one another. Besides, there is nothing you can do for Me anyway. Loving your brothers and sisters, my beloved children, is the only way you can honor Me. As Benjamin Franklin said: The most acceptable service we render to Him is in doing good to His other children."

> **"A man is born gentle and weak.**
> **At death, he is hard and stiff.**
> **Green plants are tender and filled with sap.**
> **At death, they are withered and dry.**
> **Therefore, the stiff and unbending is the disciple of death,**
> **And the gentle and yielding is the disciple of life."**
> *Lao Tzu*

Maintaining mental flexibility also broadens our ability to find unexpected moments of learning and success and, coupled with our timing, can enable us to benefit even from the most unlikely of occasions or unexpected sources of inspiration. For instance, open-minded teachers are able to improve their abilities to teach by learning from students who may pose a strange question or cause the teacher to rethink an approach to solving a problem. We call these instances "teachable moments."

A champion in the martial arts, too, must keep an open mind in order to continue to grow and progress, especially after becoming a Black Belt, because having finally achieved this rank may become an excuse for complacency. Becoming a Black Belt in a particular style of the martial arts is merely the beginning of a continuing, life-long journey of learning.

Earning a Black Belt means the individual has demonstrated proficiency in the development of basics and in numerous extensions of those basics. As with students of any other rank, Black Belts must be receptive to the lessons that their senior Black Belts may provide as well as stay sensitive to "teachable moments" that might occur when interacting with peers or more junior students.

Let us tap into our limitless potential by actualizing the principle of water and by maintaining or cultivating that open-mindedness which expands our horizons. As Lao Tzu expounded, the closed-mind is the principle of stagnation and death. To be champions in life and the martial arts, we must maintain mental and physical flexibility in order to keep our minds and bodies young and vibrant.

7. Posture/ Honesty/ Business Integrity

In martial arts, upright posture lends a balanced beauty to the art. This beauty is appreciated not only by the martial artists but also by the general public. As the standard of physical beauty—symmetry and relative proportions—is generally universal, the inner beauty of a person with good posture—correct alignment—also is universal.

The martial arts champion must develop good posture, which requires good flexibility and persistence in order to correctly align the body. Developing good posture in the martial arts has aesthetic appeal, but more importantly, it is essential for efficient and effective application of techniques—whether it is for combat (sparring or self-defense) or for performing public demonstrations. Having bad posture will hinder and weaken the power and speed of a movement, minimizing its impact.

As it is vital for martial artists, good posture is also key to becoming a champion in life. Posture is the outward manifestation of a person's character. Aligned posture represents a person's character being correct and upright through honesty, while crooked posture represents flawed character. There is a reason for the phrase "upstanding citizen" being associated with being of good character.

From a physical standpoint, developing good posture is critical for maintaining our physical youth. Posture—whether aligned or slouched—directly affects the health of our spine, which could mean the difference between aging quickly or aging gracefully. If we develop a habit of standing, sitting, and lying down in alignment with our natural spinal curvature, our spines will stay healthier and keep our bodies upright for years to come.

As aforementioned, the position of our bodies impacts our mood: when I ask my audience to physically demonstrate sadness, their bodies slouch, and when I ask them to demonstrate happiness, they become upright. In addition to improving mood, good posture improves our social status and image.

I have spent ten years researching how to invent spine-correcting shoulder straps. Children's postures are more crooked than ever due to how they sit at their computers. Some children are glued to their computers for fun and games, some are there for studies. I hope someday all governments will make an invention like the shoulder straps available for children, on whose shoulders the future of their countries must be carried.

Let us re-discover and maintain good posture, not only for our health, social standing and good looks, but also as a manifestation of our mental discipline while we develop good character through truthfulness.

Seven Qualities of a Champion

	Martial Arts	Life	Business
1	Power	Knowledge	Capital
2	Quickness	Alertness	Awareness
3	Timing	Punctuality	On-Time Delivery
4	Endurance	Perseverance	Persistence
5	Balance	Rationality	Stability
6	Flexibility	Gentleness	Adaptability
7	Posture	Honesty	Business Integrity

C. Discipline and Formality

The above Seven Qualities of a Champion are obtained through disciplined living. In order to develop these qualities, proper education along with discipline is vital. I would like to take George Washington's quote further by adding that discipline is the backbone of human society, not just the army. We must all develop a habit of taking disciplined actions in light of a positive vision because this will always give us the energy and courage necessary to act wisely.

"Small daily discipline weighs ounces; regret weighs tons." *Jim Rohn*

The crisis in American education has been of prime concern to our nation. Many have spoken and written about the decline of a constructive attitude in academics. The real concern, however, is with the decline in children's discipline at home as well as in the classrooms. The word "disciple" means "follower" or "student," and has "discipline" as its root. A good disciple comes from a good disciplined education by disciplined teachers and parents. All the problems of our society stem, not from our children, but from our leaders, parents, and teachers not setting living examples.

The purpose of self-discipline is to perfect moral and mental attitudes for proper behavior and correct actions in life. The Jhoon Rhee "Joy of Discipline" program has been created to spread this truth throughout the world. The philosophy of "Joy of Discipline" helps to develop mind/body coordination which can be applied to all areas of life.

The two most important and basic physiologies of the program are shown in the formality of "Chario" (attention) and "Kyungye" (respect). "Chario" is a Korean word – one of the two most important commands used in Taekwondo – meaning "to pay undivided attention" to teachers in order to learn a subject more effectively. Students are required to stand still during the "Chario" command until a "Shio" command—meaning "at ease" – is given. During the "Chario" stance, even if a bee were to sting you on the nose, you would not move to chase it.

"Kyungye" is another Korean command used in Taekwondo, meaning "respect" or "to bow" – universal body language which shows respect for parents, teachers, and elders. If one loves and respects teachers, he or she is inspired to learn more effectively. Students want to learn from teachers they respect. Students do not care about learning from teachers for whom they have no respect.

These two psychological basics of all learning, "Chario" and "Kyungye," are emphasized by repetition of the appropriate formal physiology. The act of standing at attention produces alertness; the physiology of bowing serves psychologically as a reminder of humility and respect, and thus is a conditioning tool for teaching a respectful state of mind. A motion triggers an emotion as much as an emotion triggers a motion.

In August 1983, I read a book called "The Making of George Washington" by General William Wilbur, a recipient of the US Congressional Medal of Honor in World War II. General Wilbur told the story that whenever Augustine Washington, George's father, walked into the house, nine year-old George always stood up. I asked myself: "How come my 16 year-old son, Chun, never does that for me?" I remembered that I used to stand up for my father in Korea.

I showed Chun the paragraph from the book and explained that, for the Father of America, George Washington's family custom was also a Korean one. I persuaded my son by saying: "It is going to be awkward at first but you will soon get used to the new way." He agreed to give it a try.

The next day, I was so anxious to see my son stand up for me. When I came home about five in the afternoon, I found Chun halfway lying on the couch, watching television. I slammed the door to make sure he heard me coming. Chun turned his head toward the door and then turned back to watch TV. He had forgotten his promise. I, however, was not totally disappointed because someone else stood up for me. Guess who that was? It was my little French poodle, Slunky.

Although I did so in my earlier years, I do not believe in yelling at others. Yelling will make a child so emotional, their reason cannot function properly. The sound waves of yelling always go into one ear and out the other. However, the soft-spoken words of wisdom go into one ear and will reach the brain. If the brain finds weight in words of profound thought, gravity will carry them down to the heart. Once they touch the heart, the child will never forget them.

I approached Chun with a smile saying: "Slunky just stood up to greet me, although he never promised me to do so." A golden rule of teaching children is, never fail to correct children's mistakes, but always with a smile until a desired habit is created in a child or student. Chun was very embarrassed because a dog had beaten him in a human behavior contest.

And to this day, my son Chun never fails to stand up when I come home. I also told him to add bowing and a hand shake with both hands. At the end of August 1985, right before Chun left for his first year in college at William & Mary, he said: "Daddy, ever since you taught me to stand up, I am closer to you than ever before. I thank you for that." That moment, I couldn't stop my tears.

East Asian people's education in self-discipline contributes to their current economic success. America taught Asians the techniques of business management, but Asians did not abandon disciplining their children as too many Americans have. It's also worth noting that many successful Asian social, business, and political leaders have learned self-discipline from martial arts—like Taekwondo, Kung Fu, Contemporary Wushu, Karate, Judo, etc.

The combined training of the body and the mind has been practiced by everyone from Buddhist monks to ancient Greek philosophers. In Greek, "gymnasium" means "high school" or "total education," not merely a place for physical training. In this traditional Western sense, Asian martial arts can be a perfect tool to help restore the discipline too often forgotten in homes and classrooms, not only for the children, but also for their parents and teachers as well. Our world today needs to be reconstructed from the top down to the bottom.

Chapter II: The Universal Purpose and Values of Life

I have been searching for the metaphysical truth about this fascinating world and our complex human nature throughout my 65 years of training in Taekwondo. Finally, what has come to me is a vision – I must promote Taekwondo everywhere around the world for the rest of my life. I am committed to actualizing this vision, by which I have been thinking, speaking, and living each day for the last 45 years.

My common sense tells me that something is very wrong with human society. Fortunately, I believe that I have discovered the major cause of the world's problems: DECEPTION motivated by self-gain. This is by itself the cause of the world's suffering.

When a national leader deceives his citizens, countless lives may be lost through unjust wars and terrible poverty can result from grossly irresponsible wasting of a nation's funds. When leaders in business deceive, we have learned that they will not only hurt their shareholders and cause their employees to become jobless; they can also lead to entire national economies becoming bankrupt. On a more individual level, when friends, family members, or neighbors deceive one another, it can tear relationships apart and even sow the seeds for future generations of bloody feuding.

I am relieved to know that deception is the only cause for the myriad of problems in human society. The root cause of all our problems is deceiving, the habit of people motivated by egotistical self-gain at the expense of their fellow men. The only way to fix this universal problem is through educating the contaminated human conscience on a global scale.

A. The Universal Purpose of Life

If the purpose of five senses of six billion people is universal, so too must be the purpose of life itself for those same six billion. Five senses are there to serve the purpose of life. Then, what is this purpose?

Children at age four or five begin to think and to question all new things they encounter with one question: "Why?" They are constantly asking the reasons or purposes for actions or phenomena. However, most people live without knowing the clear purpose of life. Without the answer to this basic question, our lives will be confused forever.

What is the difference between a person living without a purpose and a plane flying without a destination? Both have the potential to cause destruction to themselves and others. Nothing exists in our lives without a purpose; when something no longer serves our purpose, it becomes trash. Doesn't everything you own serve the purpose of your life? Then, what is the purpose of your life? No wonder some throw their lives away like trash. Isn't it a pity that we do not clearly understand the reason we are here? Parents must be prepared to answer this basic question for their children.

When I give my speeches around the world, I ask my audience, "What is the purpose of your life?" The answer must be the same for all six billion people: to recognize what are the universal human values. Establishing the universal values among all people is vital, for if all people accept certain values as being universal, this will automatically erase all the conflict. Children often can answer the purpose of life, but most adults cannot. The answer to this simple question is Happiness. Can you think of any other answer that can be agreed on by all six billion people?

B. Three Universal Values of Life

The universal purpose and values of human life are the first three things we must teach children starting at age three. Without the universal values for all six billion people, conflicts among all people are inevitable. The three universal values are TBL, which stands for Truth, Beauty, and Love. I am proud to declare these to be the universal purpose and human values upon which all six billion of us can agree.

When I ask my audiences—ranging from young children to the elderly—to recite these affirmations, they are not only able to make sense of them but are also profoundly moved by the simplicity of how the universal purpose of life is tied together by the three universal values of life.

Physical beauty can be improved with Mary Kay or Avon. However, what makes the heart beautiful? It is truth that beautifies all human hearts. Therefore, Truth is the first universal human value.

Why do people love? People fall in love with physical beauty and/or beauty of the heart. When I first saw my wife, I said to myself: "Wow! She is beautiful." I fell in love with her beauty—both inner and outer beauty. Thus, Beauty is the second universal human value.

Happiness is the universal purpose of life for all. The happiest time is when you share love with another person—spouse, family, or friend. Therefore, Love is the third universal human value.

People improve their external environment but neglect the world within: the mind. As a result, it becomes nearly impossible to find true happiness in this world. We must teach ourselves and future generations the universal purpose of life, how to achieve it, and how to enjoy developing the embodiment of the TBL values. I would like for you to say aloud the following:

> **"When I am Truthful my heart is Beautiful;**
> **When my heart is Beautiful, people Love me;**
> **When people Love me, I am Happy."**
> *Jhoon Rhee*

In contrast, distrust creates thick walls between body and mind, among individuals, groups, nations, and religions. We create not only our fences but also the guards to watch over each other.

What a waste it is! These establishments and activities waste our time and energy, enormously. And time and energy are the most precious gifts for our lives to enjoy.

The only way to eliminate these walls is by living in mutual unself-conscious trust according to TBL values. I have had the vision of such a world and tried to live by these universal good values for the last 45 years. Only these three good values of TBL will bring us happiness—The Happy Way for all. Please read aloud the following:

> **"When I deceive, my heart is ugly;**
> **When my heart is ugly, people hate me;**
> **When people hate me, I am unhappy."**
> *Jhoon Rhee*

Therefore, TBL stands for Truth, Beauty, and Love, which are the three basic GOOD values because they bring Happiness and so are best for any way of life. DUH stands for Deceiving, Ugliness, and Hatred; and these are the three basic EVIL values, because they are against our happiness. Are they not simple, obvious, and easily understood, even by children?

The philosophy understood by children may change the world; but a philosophy understood only by college graduates will not be able to change society because their consciences are already polluted by contaminated social environments.

We must always act according to TBL; and we must only be aware of evil values in order never to take actions contaminated by DUH. There is one good use for evil – to help us understand what is good. Without knowing darkness, light has no meaning. The evil values should exist only as concepts, never as possible actions.

When parents tell their children to be good, most of them will reply in the affirmative. However, a sharp child might ask: "What is good, mom?" The mom must be prepared to answer such a question. Unfortunately, I am afraid many parents do not know exactly how.

This is how you handle the question: "Would you like to be happy or unhappy?" The child will say, "Happy." "Then, would you be truthful or deceiving?" With this simple explanation of TBL, the child will understand why he or she has to be good. If all parents know how to handle such a question and live by what they teach, then, all children will become the embodiments of TBL or saints.

Therefore, one who never deceives for a few years will soon become the embodiment of TBL—the embodiment of happiness. A society of such individuals will lead to a perfect, happy society, or as I call it: TRUTOPIA.

Happy people have everything; unhappy people have nothing. A truly happy person is a being completely integrated with the cosmic mind—the collective conscience. We need only one set of rules for life's game, just as a sports game with more than one set of rules will end in chaos. Naturally, the human society with its six billion different sets of rules for the game of life cannot be orderly. One set of rules of life – TBL as good and DUH as evil – must be adopted by the world, to permanently eliminate all conflicts from this planet.

C. Definitions of GOOD and EVIL

1. Truth, beauty, and love are **GOOD** values, because they lead us to find the purpose of life, HAPPINESS.
2. Deception, ugliness and hatred are **EVIL** values because they lead us to find an unhappy life.

D. Who am I?

This is an age-old question everyone ponders at one time or another. It is a tough one to answer without knowing the purpose of life. As we grow, we ask questions about things we do not know. As children grow, they become very curious about everything they encounter for the first time. I remember asking my mother to explain everything I saw for the first time, especially, when a stranger visited our home—I sure wanted to know who this person was! Yet, we have a problem knowing who we ourselves are. Who am I? To answer this question, I would once again like to introduce:

My Four Daily Affirmations

1. I like myself because I always take action to make good things happen. (Strength)
2. I am humanly perfect because I never make a mistake knowingly. (Honesty)
3. I am wise because I always learn something good everyday. (Knowledge)
4. I am happy that I am me because I always choose to be happy. (Happiness)

Whenever a baby is born, the baby is surrounded by heaven above, earth below, and all things around the baby. Since the baby is at the center of the universe relative to the baby, and the purpose of life is happiness, the best answer to the question "Who am I?" is:

"I am one of six billion active, humanly perfect, wise, and happy centers of the universe." *Jhoon Rhee*

Each one of us was supposed to be the source of happiness for everyone else on this planet. Instead, people became the source of problems that turn us against one another because people create a world where we cannot trust one another. Therefore, our only job is reconstructing the world into an Earth where everyone can trust everyone else because children's character education begins in homes and school classrooms, while their hearts are still pure. Let us take action to make this happen.

Let us teach ourselves and future generations, not only with words, but also by adopting Lead by Example Action Philosophy before it is too late.

E. Defining Human Perfection

I defined human perfection as being an attainable goal for everyone. A perfect human being is a person who never knowingly makes a mistake. This means the first and only crime you can commit is deceiving your own conscience. Many can achieve human perfection by living according to this definition. Human perfection does not require one to be all-knowing but rather having perfection of character. When no one on this planet ever commits a crime or knowingly makes a mistake, TRUTOPIA can become reality.

We must educate our children with all our hearts and souls, by setting living examples as parents, teachers, and mentors. If all parents in homes and teachers in schools are humanly perfect today, they will produce humanly perfect political, religious, social, and business leaders sooner than we think.

Three human qualities we must develop are strength in the body, honesty in the heart, and knowledge in the mind. I have tried to live by this motto for the last 45 years. Judge what it has made of me. Everybody loves to follow a leader with these qualities. Therefore, if parents develop them and lead by example, children's physical and mental education will automatically become successful.

Chapter III: TBL – Truth, Beauty, and Love

A. Truth

Truth must be universal, unchanging, and everlasting. Truth in Washington should be truth in Moscow; the truth of 6,000 years ago should be the truth today and forever. If two countries accept the universal truth, there will be a common understanding by both countries. The day every country adopts the universal truth or mother nature's TBL, we will see the light of eternal peace, harmony, and joy of the world.

> **"Truth is conscientious common sense in agreement with nature, the laws of physics, chemistry, biology, animal instinct, conscience, reason, and emotion. Truth is nowhere but within each thing and life itself and is unchanging and everlasting regardless of time and space."** *Jhoon Rhee*

> **Money can buy weight machines but not muscles.**
> **Money can buy people but not true love or respect.**
> **Money can buy books but not wisdom.**
> **Truth will give you all the above, muscles, true love and respect, and wisdom.**

Each of us on this tiny planet was born to live in harmony with one another as a single family based on the standards of mother nature's TBL. However, humankind lost these universal values, and the importance of mutual love among all beings. Humankind has lived in pursuit of egotistical self-gain while forgetting the principle of total benefit through mutual benefit through trust.

On the other hand, some people, who understood truth and had a great passion for humankind, dedicated their lives to changing our mournful history by becoming lights of TBL. In doing so, they have guided a turbulent humanity toward the good we see today in society.

In order to become such truthful people, every cell in our body must be a healthy and ideal cell because one cancer cell could cause danger to the other 100 trillion cells in our body. By the same token, in order to achieve TRUTOPIA, each person has to be educated about how to become an ideal person of TBL.

We can begin with the Lead By Example Action Philosophy movement to make every human soul be humanly perfect. Then all the closed gates of nations and religions will open for us to visit one another freely and joyfully. The world is destined to be a perfectly happy place for all some day, and every soul must participate to strive for that day with hope. The world cannot be a happy place until all cells of the world—all people—are humanly perfect. I know there are many who say it is impossible for a person to be humanly perfect, but remember, we are only limited by the limitation of our thoughts.

The perfect world should be the only destination for world and human history. I believe that the world is already perfect except for the hearts of the people in it. The day the world begins to produce humanly perfect people will be the beginning of this new world, TRUTOPIA.

When Thomas Edison perfected the first commercially successful light bulb, millions of them were produced soon thereafter. By the same token, when the first humanly perfect person appears, soon we will have millions, then billions more to follow. The first humanly perfect person may already exist, recognizable only if you look for her or him sincerely; in fact, you may even have walked past this individual already. Within less than a hundred years, we will all recognize in each other a humanly perfect person. Thus, TRUTOPIA will be actualized within the 21st century.

Soon, I hope we will all be enlightened enough to actualize who we really are in relationship to other people and the universe at large. I hope we will all find a new hope in life and work together to build a new world of TBL among all people.

We must start with the children. As children are growing into adulthood, they can be shaped in many ways. Their bodily growth affects them, of course. Their muscles and nervous system are maturing toward adulthood. The people around children—parents, teachers, peers, and other role models—must lead by example. Children are learning their identity and self-worth from observing and interacting with the people around them. People make many mistakes, but among them all, nothing is worse than neglecting our children's upbringing and education—physical, character, and intellectual education.

> **"It takes a year to harvest a crop, ten years to see the full beauty of a tree, and fifty years to make a person."** *Korean Proverb*

Knowing who you are to yourself and to other people is the most important knowledge of all. The feeling of what you think you are worth as a person is called your sense of "self-worth." This world often makes you think less of yourself than you deserve. Many people have problems because they have not developed a habit of choosing to be positive and happy all the time. People often find themselves unhappy because they choose to be unhappy.

Instead of choosing to be unhappy by default, we should choose to be happy by thinking, visualizing, and acting positively. Remember, the environment of your outward world is a reflection of you—the world within. When you are happy, the world appears happy; when you are miserable, the world around you seems miserable. So, let us brighten the world by brightening our hearts consciously and choosing to be happy.

B. Beauty

Beauty causes lovely emotions. This universe consists of beautiful stars in heaven, beautiful minerals, plants, animals, and the people on this globe. All things of Earth are beautiful—the sky is beautiful; mountains are beautiful; oceans are beautiful; trees, birds, fish, animals, and people are beautiful.

There are two kinds of human beauty: physical beauty and heart beauty. When I ask groups of five year-old children, "What is more important – physical beauty or heart beauty?" Everybody shouts in unison, "Heart beauty, sir!"

Let's say, your spouse has been beautiful for the last fifty years, ever since you met. One day, you catch your spouse deceiving you in a serious matter. Will she ever be as beautiful again? Thus, the only thing that threatens human society's vision of TRUTOPIA is ugliness in the heart.

In order to cultivate beauty of the heart, we must be truthful with ourselves and each other. When people have beautiful hearts, that beauty radiates outward and enhances our perception of their physical appearance. Therefore, beauty is a product of being truthful.

C. Love

It is absolutely true that love is the cause of our happiest emotion. Love is the reason we live because we cannot find happiness without love. We love our children unconditionally, but more importantly, we should love ourselves because we cannot love others without loving ourselves first.

If we do not love ourselves, we are mentally telling ourselves that we are unworthy of love. This would be the message conveyed to those around us. In that case, why would they feel any differently than we do about ourselves? How can we know what love is if we do not possess a sense of self-worth? That is why we must learn to value ourselves with love and set an example for those around us—especially our children.

Let us make our hearts beautiful by being truthful. When we are truthful to ourselves, we tell our conscience that we are worthy of trust, which builds our self-esteem. When we are truthful to ourselves and others, then our hearts become beautiful. With our beautiful hearts, we make ourselves magnets for love from others. Therefore, love is a product of beauty of the heart, and being loved by oneself and others brings us happiness!

D. Creative Evolution of the Universe

There have been two schools of thought, Creationism and Evolutionism. I have a happy solution to satisfy both schools of thoughts: Creative Evolution of the Universe.

The universe was created by mother nature's TBL and has evolved into the dwelling place of all tangible things and all living beings. Nothing can evolve without a seed or thought first having been created by some cosmic mind. So this universe has been created by thoughts or ideas of TBL: the universal values of Truth, Beauty, and Love.

In order to create beans, we must have seeds to be planted. The seeds will grow or evolve in time to produce the crops. We the people make things happen. Can we do anything without first conceiving the thought of what we want to do? From the above reasoning, Creative Evolution of the Universe is the happy solution for two different schools of thought

Just as we, in order to create things, must first have clear ideas, so, too, does the Cosmic Mind contain perfect ideas of truth, beauty, and love, to create the mineral kingdom, plant kingdom, and animal kingdom. For example, it is interesting to find Truth values – science – in the mineral kingdom; Truth + Beauty values in the plant kingdom; and Truth + Beauty + Love values in the animal kingdom, as shown in the diagram below:

The ideas of TBL values (center of the diagram) created the Energy, first, (top center of the diagram). If you follow around the circle clock-wise, you see that the purpose of energy is Motion; the purpose of motion is Heat; the purpose of Heat is Light. The purpose of energy, motion, heat, and light is to create an environment containing Gases, Liquids, and Solids. The purpose of all of the above, of this changing from Energy to Solids, is to create an environment fit for plants, animals, and human beings.

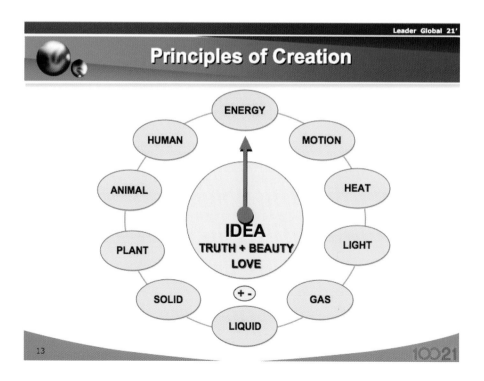

Principles of Creation

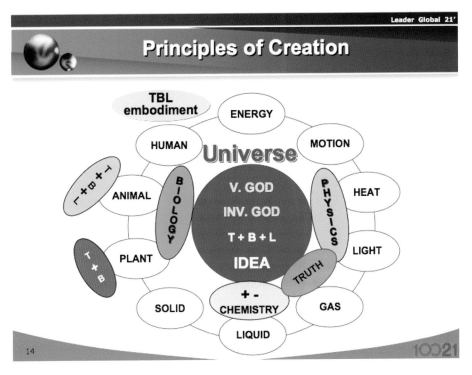

I believe we the people of the universe were supposed to become the embodiment of TBL; we were always meant to reflect the original creative ideas – Truth, Beauty, and Love for mankind. Instead, we became the people of deceiving, ugliness, and hatred, and we have created a human society where everyone is doomed to deceive, be ugly, and hate one another, to kill, be unhappy, and cry.

Are we normal or insane?

E. Might for Right

"Might for Right" has been the motto of the Jhoon Rhee Institute of Taekwondo since its founding in 1962. This motto refers to a theme echoed in history: "right" meant "righteous" and "left" meant "sinister" in languages such as Russian, Spanish, German, Korean, and others. Of course, this doesn't really mean that left-handed people are evil. My son Jimmy is left-handed and is a very good and wise son.

As it is mentioned earlier in this book, I wrote the following narration in 1968, a little over 40 years ago, to describe the Jhoon Rhee Martial Arts philosophy, "Might for Right," by reciting this lyric to the motion picture theme song from "Exodus."

"Might For Right"

In the beginning, when the universe was created, the energy of God swept across
the great void in a definite direction. Truth, Beauty, and Love (TBL) manifested
through all things of His creation. Then He molded His crowning achievements,
His beloved children: man and woman.

Since then, one strange element that has remained a mystery crept into the midst
of all mankind: the evil force: Deceiving, Ugliness, and Hatred (DUH).
Let us make the left hand a symbol of that evil. As the sinister left hand covers
the righteous right, so has evil tried to destroy the good, just as Cain murdered Abel at the
beginning of history.

From that time on, the history of mankind has known a constant conflict between
good and evil, as the righteous right and the sinister left clash against each other.
It is our only hope that the absolute power of His Love and our actions can
someday bring an eternal end to evil.

There shall be no more Deceiving, no more Ugliness, no more Hatred.
There will come a time when all mankind will live in peace and happiness on this earth.
As Truth, Beauty, and Love cast all the evil elements out of this universe,
so does the righteous right cover the evil left: Might for Right.

Chapter IV: My Vision for the 21st Century

A. What is Vision?

1. Defining "Visionary"

    A visionary is one who can see in his or her imagination the unseen and the potential. Every one of us is born with the ability to become a visionary, possessing within ourselves and the world we live in, the potential to make history and save the world. What could be more noble than a visionary who seeks a way to make this world a happier place for all six billion people to live?

    Although you did not come into this world by your choice, you have been given the right to choose every thought that forges your behaviors and actions in your daily life. What you think is what you are; you will become what you think, speak, and do repeatedly. Your thoughts of the past made you what you are today; your thoughts of today will take you to some place tomorrow.

    You are the result of all your thoughts throughout your life. A sweet thought of TBL will result in a happy emotion; a bitter thought of DUH, an unhappy state of mind. Either way, you are the sole owner of the right to make a choice. It is obvious that Happiness is the natural choice for everyone.

    No matter how wild a vision may be, it is invaluable when it becomes a reality, for all visions seem wild at the beginning. Throughout history, the world is always being made more beautiful by the devotion of a few people with revolutionary visions. Those who conceive a beautiful and noble vision will actualize their dreams and find joy from it.

2. Envisioning Noble Visions

    To envision is to plant the seeds of realization; to desire is to nourish achievement.

    People can achieve as far as their visions reach. Seeing is believing; believing is seeing. Therefore, a vision can lead to a reality through never-ending actions done until it comes true. As long as a vision stays alive enough to generate energy for action, it will become a reality through consistent and conscientious efforts. In this way, our visions of TRUTOPIA will lead to a world more enlightened, more beautiful, and happier for all.

    This vision of a happy world showed me that everyone on this planet could be truthful, beautiful, and lovingly happy with every breath of life. You must visualize yourself as a happy person. You are a small universe of TBL, created to reflect this universe which also is made from the energy of TBL. One noble vision gives birth to another for as long as it lives in your heart. Your vision is your hope and a promise made to yourself and your posterity; your dream is the prophecy you will someday realize.

Life's stubborn circumstances test you, to find out the degree of clarity of your vision. Do not fail the test; keep your vision alive, brighter and larger, by your unprecedented conviction. Then, the negative circumstances will soon yield and bring you new, positive circumstances which will permit your vision to become a reality.

As a diamond is a piece of coal made tough and beautiful under pressure, you can become a guiding light for people by your enduring patience. My dominant vision for over 45 years has been to help create this coming world in which "everyone is happy with every breath of life." This vision may seem too far-fetched to be accepted by anyone today, but, remember, a vision is an art of seeing the invisible.

Developing a vision will help you to see the potentials which have not yet become realities. Your internal actions, your thoughts, will soon transform into external actions to bring your visions into reality. You will become the visionary you honor in your heart and the idea you nurture in your mind. Imagine a noble vision and let it be alive with absolute conviction in your heart, it will bring much joy to you and fellow humans sooner than you think.

A person with a noble vision shines as one who is in touch with divine wisdom. If knowledge is like the wave of an ocean, wisdom is the ocean. Knowledge accumulates from reading, listening, watching, observing, or interacting with the world. Wisdom enlightens within a person of noble visions by living the truth with conviction.

3. Actualizing Visions into Reality

Achievements and failures of your vision are the results of your actions; you are the only master when it comes to actualizing your vision. Your pain and pleasure also result from actions caused by your vision. You become what you envision and how you act.

As a diamond is found in deep mines, wisdom is hidden in the deep mine of your mind. The mind is like a garden where beautiful flowers blossom as the result of seeds sewn by the gardener. If the gardener neglects his responsibility, it will become the ground for ugly weeds. You are the gardener for the garden of your mind, which will be filled with the seeds of either a positive vision or of gloomy thoughts.

A thought dictates behavior, behavior creates a habit, and habits shape destiny. Therefore, the first step for a thousand-mile journey is a thought.

As the flowers in a garden never could blossom without the seed, good or evil acts never could have been executed without a seed of thought, regardless of whether the action is done consciously or by accident. As no wise gardener will sow the seeds of weeds, the wise do not permit impure thoughts to slip into their minds.

Follow only your conscience, to become a divine human being. The heart must be governed by TBL, to guard tightly against the invasion of the dangerous triad of DUH. All achievements, whether they are personal or collective, are the results of the vision and actions of the achievers. What counts at the end is your objective. What does the success intend? Is it a selfish result, a collective one, or both?

A wise person links all visions to the purpose of life. Without this connection, all the successes are meaningless. Purposelessness is not only a waste but is a vice which eventually leads to a dead end. A person without a purpose in life, lives with fear and worry over trivial matters. A purpose in life gives us the energy to get up again whenever we fall down.

Living with deceitful, ugly, and hateful thoughts is the quickest way to invite diseases. On the other hand, a life of beautiful thoughts and beautiful exercise, such as performing a martial ballet, will keep the body youthful well past age 100. Negative DUH thoughts can drain a person's life-span. Quality of living through TBL builds up one's natural immunity and acts as a powerful form of preventative medicine.

Health and sickness are both rooted in emotions, which are caused by thoughts chosen by oneself. Clean living is the way to a joyful life in a healthy body. To have a healthy body, choose to be happy with every breath of life. Thoughts of DUH rob the body of its youth and health; thoughts of TBL deliver abundant energy for a healthy and happy life.

I have repeatedly said the purpose of life is to be happy. There is a way we all can be happy all the time – by our choices, by reminding ourselves that "Everything Happens for the Best." In the words of singer Bobby McFerin, "Don't worry; be happy." For effective motivation, we should never try to motivate people out of fear, only with hope.

I used to fly to Tampa twice a year to test my students at Jhoon Rhee Schools in Tampa. I did not have to fly the day that Florida Airline Flight 80 crashed into the Potomac River in the 1980s. Imagine if I were scheduled to fly that day and missed the flight by five seconds, I may initially have been frustrated and disappointed.

Then, just as I was driving back home, imagine how I would have felt upon hearing the news that very flight I missed fell into the Potomac River, killing more than 60 people. The same fact—missing the flight—could be interpreted as a terrible thing, at one moment, or a wonderful thing, in different circumstances. If I were to have made it on-time to that flight, I would not be here to write this book.

I had a friend who was upset because he was fired from a job paying him $50,000 a year in 1990. He asked for my help to find a new job. I told him not to worry because "Everything happens for the best." Two weeks later, I called my friend to tell him I found a job for him paying $60,000 a year. He thanked me, but explained that just two days before, he had found a job himself—paying $100,000 a year! If he had not been fired, he never would have looked for the job paying him twice as much.

What you envision, you achieve. Every person has his or her own key to open the door of wishes, just as we also hold the saw to cut the chain of bad habits. People are the masters of their own joy and sorrow. The wise choose joy; the foolish invite pain. The wise share their joy with others, which creates more joy; the foolish share their pain and only cause more pain.

The wise are made joyful by the joy of others; the foolish are made unhappy by the joy of others and feel happy only about others' pain. The wise know the purpose of life is happiness. Such is the true master who understands truth without being clouded by individual subjectivities of reality. A small seed of noble vision often takes root there and grows to bear healthy fruits. Those who run toward a positive vision will find TRUTOPIA, and there, find everlasting happiness.

B. Envision all Conflicts Fading Away

Human history—including in the US—has been a story of constant conflict plagued by the evil institution of slavery. For much of human history, there existed the fear of punishment by dictators. We also admit, every dictatorship lived with constant fear of being overthrown by its own people.

There are generally three reasons for conflict among individuals, groups, countries, and religions – conflict of ideology, conflict of interest, and conflict of emotion. The three universal values, TBL, are the solution to all three conflicts. If two parties share the same Truth, conflict of ideology will not exist. If two parties share the same Beauty in their hearts, conflict of interest will not exist. If two parties share the same Love feeling, conflict of emotion will not exist.

If we all successfully educate people to live the Lead By Example Action Philosophy, decontamination of the human heart will become a reality. In turn, decontamination of the human heart will cleanse the air, water, soil, food, and all diseases caused by DUH. Our beautiful planet will be purified of suffering by the purification of human character. I say once again, TRUTOPIA will appear as soon as all people become the embodiment of TBL. If you see this vision as I see, you will find there is nothing else to do other than committing your life to this cause.

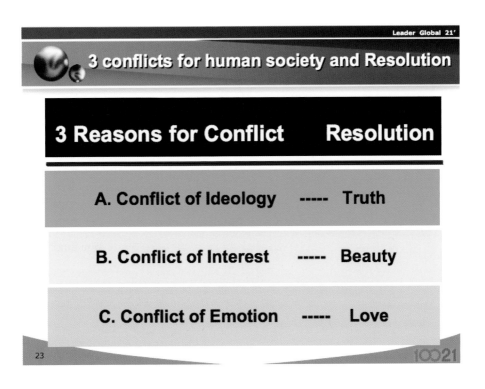

3 conflicts for human society and Resolution

3 Reasons for Conflict   Resolution

A. Conflict of Ideology   ----- Truth

B. Conflict of Interest   ----- Beauty

C. Conflict of Emotion   ----- Love

23   10021

C. Envision Everyone Living in Wealth

Everyone is literally more than a billionaire, for we are born with a bio-computer—the brain—which cannot be reproduced for a billion dollars. It is truly an amazing and valuable part of our existence. Although everyone is born to create and to perform a variety of arts for happiness, every one of us is kept too busy working just to protect ourselves against each other's invasions. We do not have time to enjoy a luxurious lifestyle because distrust causes us to waste precious time and energy.

Fortunately, however, there is hope: TRUTOPIA. In a world where all are truthful, there would be no need for unnecessary protective jobs – law, government, the military, and many fields of medicine. This would enable all to devote their extra time and energy during their non-working awake hours to the things they truly love doing: creating and performing arts. Obesity and other health concerns will not be a problem because TRUTOPIA will be clean and full of natural, high-quality food—both making it easier to go outside to exercise and to eat a healthy diet. The result will be a stress-free society, which will make its citizens healthy.

Furthermore, with this concentration of human resources being made available to the most essential of professions for living, the potential for everyone to live truly wealthy lives can become a reality. Let us look back at history and see how this can come about. In 1929, there were about 30 million farmers to feed about 100 million American people. Today, there are only three million farmers who produce food to feed 300 million people in America plus people from other countries because of advances in technology.

If one farmer works eight hours to produce food for 100 people, then one dress maker working for eight hours can manufacture clothing for 100 people. This will be much easier because we do not consume clothes everyday as we do consume food. The same would apply to a home builder who works to build and maintain housing—including plumbing, electricity, waste management, power production (clean, renewable energy) for 100 people. One more worker for another eight hours will produce every other essential. Progress in technology has made it possible for us to work dramatically fewer hours and yet still be able to produce the same amount of materials.

These technological advances must continue, using clean, renewable energy because the health of our bodies is tied to the health of our planet. If the air, water, and land we walk on becomes saturated with contamination, then our health will fail as well. As we continue to pollute the environment with fossil fuels and other forms of environmentally toxic by-products of finite energy sources, our earth will become too toxic for us to prosper in good health. As we must cultivate strength in our bodies by keeping it clean and free of pollutants like cigarette smoke and illicit drugs, we too must do the same for our mother earth. Maintaining the health of our own bodies is in microcosm, an example of how we should treat our surrounding global environment.

With the continued pace of improvements and advancements in mass production technology, as well as the elimination of unnecessary occupations, four percent of our current population will be able to produce all the food, housing, clothing, and other necessary items for all 300 million Americans today. Of course, all of the required working hours would have to be distributed evenly among all adults, excluding the elderly and the physically unable. However, it will be possible for everyone in TRUTOPIA to work for a few hours and still maintain an efficient, clean, and self-sustaining society. Thus, they will have ample amounts of time to pursue their true passion: the arts!

Leader Global 21'

Number of US Farmers	US Populations	
Year 1929 30 Million Farmers fed 100 Million (One fed 3 or 4)		
Year 2000 3 Million Farmers fed 300 Million (One fed 100)		
1-8 hr. Farmer	Food	100
1-8 hr. Maker	Clothing	100
1-8 hr. Builder	Housing	100
1-8 hr. Worker	Everything Else	100
4x8 hr. Workers	Everything	100

In the United States of America

1 farmer works 8 hours to produce food for 100 people
1 tailor works 8 hours to produce clothes for 100 people
1 builder works 8 hours to produce housing for 100 people
1 scientist works 8 hours to produce everything else for 100 people

4 laborers x 8 hours = 32 hours
32 hours x 60 minutes = 1,920 minutes
32 hours ÷ 4 = 8 hours
1,920 minutes ÷ 100 people = 19 minutes per person

Since there are seniors and children who cannot work as productively, we can conservatively estimate 1 hour per person among those who can work.

1 hour to work…
8 hours for sleeping and personal hygiene…
How would you spend the remaining 15 hours?

D. Envision a Happy World for Everyone

Egotistical self-interest is at the root of dishonesty, which is the cause of all social problems. The resulting distrust is forcing everyone to build walls, to feel alienated and always on guard against other individuals, families, organizations, nations, and religions. When we educate our children to live only in TBL, all the problems that are destroying our society will surely fade away.

"If all men were angels, no government would be necessary." *James Madison*

When everyone on this planet is perfect in character, then military, police, intelligence, nearly all government occupations, law firms, accounting firms, locksmiths, security professions, people's character-building institutions, and many other service professions will not be necessary. These professions are the result of societies where cheating exists. In TRUTOPIA, where everyone can trust each other, there will be no need to protect oneself against other people or to worry about physical, legal, or other forms of interpersonal conflict.

When global TRUTOPIA is actualized, every social problem, such as hunger, disease, conflict, and deception, will all disappear, including even rush hour traffic jams. After increasing technology in clean energy production combines with fewer hours for work, we will not need so many cars on the road. I envision every street will have enough cars for people to drive. No one has to own a car because TRUTOPIA will be a society of Free Common Possessionism. When people leave their houses to go to a distant place, beautiful cars will be there waiting to be driven. People can pick any car, drive to their destination, and park it properly. Since everyone will be humanly perfect, people will be considerate of the next possible person's desire to drive it comfortably. When people return home, they can pick a different car of choice. So since there will be far fewer hours to work, there will be no rush hours.

Who will repair the cars that break down? There will be people who love to repair and even redesign cars to serve others, to be happy. In TRUTOPIA, everyone is an artist of his or her choice because we are born to perform some sort of art to enjoy life. Those who love nature and raising great-tasting produce and high-quality livestock will serve others to be happy by working on farms; others will pursue the culinary arts to serve others, to be happy; others will turn to fashion to make clothing to serve others, to be happy; other innovators will invent new things to serve others, to be happy; others will turn to the performing arts to serve others, to be happy. This would result in Free Common Possessionism—where everyone creates things to share with others because everyone will trust and love one another.

Free Common Possessionism is not to be confused with communism, where those at the top of the ruling party had all of the power while the vast majority of the people equally lived in poverty. Communism failed in the USSR not because the political system was wrong but because of greedy human nature motivated by selfishness—the people could not stand being equally poor in the face of well-to-do members of the central government.

TRUTOPIA is a community that practices Free Common Possessionism, where there is no need for a ruling government. I say again: when everyone in the world is humanly perfect, there will be no lawyers, government officials, defense contractors, military, police, accountants, and locksmiths because these professions are to watch deceivers and do not produce anything. Currently, however, people all over the world are busy watching and guarding against one another's intrusion, attack, deception, and other forms of evil among brothers and sisters in a family, among people in a country, and among nations in this world.

In contrast, TRUTOPIA is a society in which everybody loves everyone else instead of everybody guarding against others as our society always has to do. This means people will trust one another, thereby, eliminating all of the unnecessary jobs created to watch deceivers. With so much free time resulting, people, as Thomas Jefferson wrote, will be able to realize "life, liberty, and the pursuit of happiness."

E. Envision the World of Performing Arts for Happy Living

We will cook and eat, make dresses, build homes, and invent new things. The one hour of work is also a form of art; for farming, dress making, and building homes are forms of art.

How will people spend their 15 hours of free time each day? They will sing, dance, paint, play music and sports, innovate, and watch others performing arts. When we find such a world, we will enjoy performing or creating all kinds of art everyday. We will never have to work long hours as slaves to our own lives. Today, most of us are slaves to unnatural and complicated social structures that have been inherited and perpetuated by us. We are not stuck with this world; we surely can change it into what we envision: TRUTOPIA.

I am very hopeful because the one-hour workday vision would give every one of us a great incentive to be honest. In this vision, if everyone were honest, TRUTOPIA would become a universal reality. And yet what could be more idealistic as well as pragmatic than this vision? I am undoubtedly sure the one-hour workday is possible and will be actualized during the 21st Century.

My vision of TRUTOPIA is a message which will bring, not only unity among all people, but also harmony in diversity to reconstruct a beautiful and perfectly happy global society for people endowed with Simple Truth as the standard for universal harmony. We, the people of the world, still have a choice between inviting a catastrophe or reconstructing our planet into a perfectly happy world. TRUTOPIA will be realized through successful character education which will teach all children to believe that they are created to grow into humanly perfect beings who never make a mistake knowingly. We must teach our children with all our hearts and souls by setting our living examples. Interestingly, what John Adams wrote supports my vision:

> "Politics are divine sciences after all. The science of government is my duty to study. I must study politics and war, that my sons may have liberty to study mathematics, philosophy. My sons ought to study mathematics and philosophy, geography, natural history, commerce and agriculture, in order to give their children a right to study painting, poetry, music, architecture, statuary, tapestry, and porcelain."
>
> *John Adams*

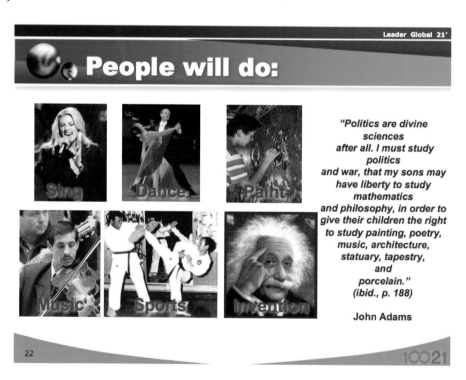

Chapter V: Second Wind of Life

I was born unhealthy in 1931, very weak and uncoordinated. Whenever I ran track in my elementary school, I was always the last one to finish. When I was six, any five year-old girl could beat me up. I thought it would be a shame to leave this world without living a healthy and happy life. If you know it is your choice, why not choose to live a healthy, wealthy, and happy life?

As I get older, my mind has been mature enough for me to choose for my life to be a happy one. I had to ask myself, how can I possibly find a happy life in this world of distrust? If nobody enjoys swimming in a contaminated pool, then how can any of us fully enjoy our lives in a world caused by contaminated human hearts?

To actualize TRUTOPIA, we must cultivate human perfection within ourselves, which means strengthening the body and purifying our hearts. As I have spoken about the importance of TBL in perfecting our hearts, I would also like to talk about the vital importance of establishing and maintaining physical and mental vitality in our health.

A. Heart Surgery and a Stroke

Unexpectedly, I had to go through eleven hours of heart surgery on February 11, 2004, at age 73. I had been living with a heart murmur ever since I was born. From 1985 until three days before the surgery, my daily exercise program, besides Taekwondo, included 1,000 push-ups. When I was discharged from the hospital, I was told that I had suffered a stroke during surgery. My wife, Theresa, had to help me put on my clothes and even to move around the house.

Two years later, I had recovered well enough to be able to break boards and do 100 push-ups in 62 seconds. I was able to do 100 push-ups in 57 seconds prior to the surgery. I was told that everyone in the Jhoon Rhee organization, including my wife and children, thought that the old Jhoon Rhee was finished. Interestingly, I was the only one who never thought I was going to die. Perhaps this is another example of how what we envision comes true. After all, I have been telling my audiences and myself that I was going to live at least 136 years ever since the early 1970s!

B. My Commitment to Live at Least 136 Years

I watched an episode of the CBS news show, 60 Minutes, which showed Ed Bradley interviewing a 109 year-old man. The old man was taking a cold bath in a creek during a very cold winter of fifteen degrees below zero in Belieze, Georgia (then part of the USSR). Ed Bradley asked the old man: "What are you doing in this cold?" He replied: "I am cleaning up to attend my mother's birthday party." Then, the TV screen showed her – a 135 year-old lady drinking and dancing.

At that moment, I said to myself, "If she can live to 135 years old, I can live at least one year more, to be 136." Ever since then, I have been saying that I will live to be at least 136 whenever I give a speech. Tens of billions of my brain cells have been hearing me say that I was going to live at least 136 years for more than three decades.

I figured out the reason why I made it through my stroke was that the fear of death never entered my mind. One day I dreamed a scene where billions of my brain cells lined up neatly like Taekwondo students and reported to me as follows: "Yes, Sir, as you ordered us to live at least 136 years, we are going to live at least 136 years, Sir."

My doctor told me that I should not fly for at least four years. The fifth anniversary of my stroke was on February 12, 2009. During these last five years, I have been to Korea 14 times and seven times to the former Soviet Union. I told myself that I may die in an airplane or while delivering my messages around the world, but I will never die in my bed.

Knowing in my heart so clearly what I have been thinking, saying, and living with such untiring enthusiasm during the last 45 years, I know that I can accomplish this personal goal of living to be at least 136 years as a step towards seeing TRUTOPIA come true. In this same spirit, I invite you to join me on the journey to perfecting ourselves and building TRUTOPIA.

C. Four Keys to Physical Health

I would like to share four tenets to good health which I have followed in maintaining my own health for the past 80 years: proper diet, proper rest, proper exercise, and positive emotions.

1. Proper diet

    a. Over Eating is Damaging
        Develop a habit of putting your fork down as soon as you feel you are not hungry. It is too late once you are full. When you are full, you have already harmed your health by overburdening your digestive system. This habit is most valuable to avoid being over-weight and for longevity, especially for senior citizens.

    b. Never Eat Prior to Bedtime
        Making love consumes more energy than any other activity. The next in line is digesting food. When you go to bed with a full stomach, you feel very tired in the morning because, instead of resting, you had to labor all night to digest.

    c. Eat Plenty of Vegetables and Fruits
        Meat is dead food, whereas fruits and vegetables are still living foods. For protein, nuts, beans, and fish are easier to digest than the protein in meat from mammals.

d. Drink at Least Half a Gallon of Water Each Day

As we take a shower to clean our skin and hair, your internal organs must take showers of their own. Drinking clean water helps our bodies to detoxify and flush waste materials out of our internal organs via urine. Make sure you do not drink too much water during your meals because it hampers the ability of our natural acids in the stomach from digesting our food. It is best to drink between your meals.

Congressman Jesse Jackson, Jr. earned his Black Belt in Taekwondo in one year and three months. He lost over 30 pounds three months prior to his Black Belt testing, which he completed on July 23, 2001. He attributed this to drinking lots of water everyday for three months. Furthermore, drinking water can help to minimize appetite—a key toward losing and maintaining a healthy weight.

2. Proper Rest

a. Good Deep Sleep

Sleep short but deep. If you do not get deep sleep, either you had an easy day, you slept too much the previous night, or else you had too much on your mind before going to sleep. Never worry; instead, tell yourself everything happens for the best. I would like once again to share a story that will convince you everything happens for the best. Let's assume you missed a plane because you were caught for speeding on the way to the airport. The plane you were supposed to take crashed during take-off and everyone in the plane was killed. Aren't you lucky? You saved your life because you were caught by the police. This happens all the time in our lives, so "Don't worry. Be happy."

b. Bed and Pillow

There were not too many spine patients in old-time Korea; everybody slept on hard floors because nobody had soft and comfortable beds. Today, there are so many spine patients, since people have begun to use soft beds. I recommend sleeping on hard mattresses and low pillows, or no pillow at all, to keep your spine straight.

c. Sleeping on Your Back

Develop a habit of sleeping on your back. Your spine can be damaged by any other position. By the same token, please try to develop the habit of sitting and walking straight all the time. Whenever I walk downtown, I always check my posture in the shop windows. There are two kinds of habits; one is good habits which can be developed only through consistent efforts, and the other is bad habits, which are automatically created by neglecting to do better.

3.   Proper Exercise

As we get older, we need to exercise regularly. As we age, most aches are caused by lack of movement.

Theresa Rhee and I married when she was 51. Ever since, we have been exercising one or two hours together daily. She lost ten pounds, and all the aching and colds she used to have throughout the year disappeared in six months. I have the "Second Wind of Life" exercise program on my DVD, which will be available for all our members of the 10021 Club International. You can contact us through the email we shared earlier.

4.   Positive Emotions

If you live with the thoughts of only TBL, you will be living with only positive emotions. Positive emotions, created by living solely with TBL, produce beta-endorphins, which support a strong immune system; whereas negative emotions, created by living with DUH, produce excessive cortisol, which suppresses the body's immune system.

D. Four Keys to Mental Health

In order to be a healthy person, we must be healthy mentally as well as physically. As I have mentioned, the four keys to physical health are proper diet, proper rest, proper exercise, and positive emotions. The four keys to our mental health are a wisdom-learning habit, a meditating habit, a creative habit, and carrying around positive emotions 24 hours every day by living nothing except TBL.

1.   Proper Diet of Words of Wisdom

We must take in the mental food that nurtures our minds. We must take in words of wisdom, not just to know worldly matters, but also to practice our daily living in Truth. I suggest everyone read many different kinds of philosophy, not only books on your own religion, but also books about other religions, for a better understanding of the rich diversity within humanity.

2.   Proper Rest Through Meditation

My definition of meditation is being in touch with my own self by breathing consciously with my eyes closed. The reason for closing my eyes is that when my eyes are open, my mind is occupied not with me but the object that is seen.

When I sleep, my physical body will rest but not my mind. For this reason, I sometimes have dreams or nightmares. My body is resting but my mind is not. Therefore, the only way to relax my mind is through meditation. I must meditate daily to relax my mind, just as I sleep daily to rest my body.

There are two parts of me, my mind - thinking Jhoon Rhee, and my body - the active Jhoon Rhee, who is constantly moving. Although most of the time I breath unconsciously, when I breath consciously, my mind and body are as one, or I am with myself alone, during which time my mind can relax very well.

After long hours of work each day, a good time to rest my body is when I am with my loved ones. Furthermore, even a better way to rest my body is to be by myself. I am one with myself when I breath consciously, for my breath is my life.

My best times to meditate are when I retire at the end of each evening, and when I awake the next morning. I can relax my mind best when my body is in its most relaxed position - when I am lying on my bed.

To meditate, close your eyes and breath in or inhale for 4 seconds and exhale for 4 seconds to start and gradually increase it to 5, 6, 7 even up to 8 seconds. When you meditate this way, you will experience more saliva being produced and are to swallow as it accumulates. You will experience a deeper and more sound sleep as you get used to it. Please repeat the same procedure as soon as you wake up in the morning.

3. Mental Exercise Through Creativity

Creativity is one of the best forms of mental exercise. Creativity can be manifested through inventions, writing, painting, composing, choreographing, research, and all sorts of performing arts. They are the best mental exercises to keep our minds alert and bodies sharp. Generally speaking, the more we use our minds and bodies, the sharper they get. Therefore, in order to keep our minds and bodies sharp, we never should stop thinking and moving. When we are creating something, we are performing one of the arts as well as providing our minds excellent exercise.

4. Positive Emotions

Not only do positive emotions affect our physical health, they also have a tremendous impact on our mental health. Staying with positive thoughts will shape the way you approach life. You can choose to be happy or miserable. Focusing on the big picture of life keeps us from letting minor annoyances bother us. The slogan of my famous "Nobody Bothers Me" TV commercials advanced my attitude to "Nothing Bothers Me." When you live with the thoughts of TBL, the three basic universal human values, your mind will be positive automatically.

E. 10021 Club International

We formed the 10021 Club International on March 4, 2002 in Seoul, Korea. The club's purpose is to create TRUTOPIA out of this insane world with the help of our Lead by Example Action Philosophy. My skeptics say, "Only an insane person can think of such an insane idea." My answer is simply, what else can I do when my vision of TRUTOPIA is so absolute?

The number 10021 originated from my life motto, "100 Years of Wisdom in a Body 21 Years Young." This does not mean a person has to be literally 21 years young, but rather, the person must have the physical characteristics of a vibrant youth even well into our 90s. I decided to make myself, not only a character role model, but also a physical role model, not only for the younger students, but also for members of Congress and all the senior citizens around the world.

I am a firm believer that people will become whatever they think, speak, and do repeatedly. That is why I decided to apply my health management know-how for more than 45 years. When I first declared the motto in my 30s, everybody laughed, but today, 45 years later, the same people are beginning to give me the benefit of the doubt.

This motto, "100 Years of Wisdom in a Body 21 Years Young," is meant to emphasize the importance of good character in a strong and healthy body. I use the word "honesty" to symbolize the prerequisite for a healthy and wise person.

"The first chapter in the book of Wisdom is Honesty." *Thomas Jefferson*

It is medically proven that humans can live an average of 120 years if we live a healthy lifestyle. The reason we are not living up to our full potential is stress, mainly caused by violating the basic principles due to living daily in a deceitful social environment where everybody has to be on guard against everybody else. Therefore, I created the 10021 Club International that stands for "100 Years of Wisdom in a Body 21 Years Young."

The even more profound meaning of 10021 is to complete TRUTOPIA during the 100 years of the 21st century. I define wisdom as an ability to recognize the true value of things and ideas. What could be a more valuable idea than achieving happy TRUTOPIA and recreating everyone there as a person of 100 years of wisdom in a body of 21 years young?

I have described the ways to achieve and maintain physical and mental health, not only to improve and lengthen our own lives, but also to prepare ourselves to be humanly perfect. In addition to knowledge in the mind and honesty in the heart, let us strengthen our bodies first.

Chapter VI: A Plan of Action

A. Jeju-do

In order to make a global vision come true, first, one must have the idea, and second, one must have a plan of action. The idea is to make everyone on this planet happy with every breath of life. My plan of action is to follow the universal creative principle by growing from simple to complicated, from one person to billions, from one school to millions of schools, one city to thousands of cities, one nation to hundreds of nations, and finally, to achieve one happy global society.

For decades, I have been looking for a small-size province to be the first model TRUTOPIA. I have finally found an opportunity with the beautiful South Korean Island called Jeju-do. It is located a few miles off the southwestern tip of South Korea's mainland. Jeju-do is an ideal place to test the TRUTOPIA action philosophy, because the size of the land and population is just right. Jeju-do has a little over a half million people—one percent of South Korea's population of 50 million. It will be easier to test the TRUTOPIA action philosophy with a half million people than with 50 million.

Furthermore, I found a Bonsai garden in Jeju-do so beautiful that it can be seen as a physical model for the entire "global garden of TRUTOPIA." The garden, called "Thinking Garden," was built by Mr. Sung, Bum Young, a good friend and the garden's owner. The Garden has been visited by leaders of different countries such as Hu Jintao of the People's Republic of China and others. Mr. Sung received many letters of admiration from those visitors.

I have been proposing the TRUTOPIA idea to the people of Jeju-do ever since 2001. Then, interestingly enough, the South Korean government announced Jeju-do to be a self-governing and visa-free province in 2007. This means Jeju-do can create its own educational policy based on a pilot program to teach Lead by Example Action Philosophy. I have given a number of speeches in Jeju-do and shared LEAP philosophy with students of elementary, middle, and high schools, colleges, universities, and many social groups around the island.

To illustrate how I will create TRUTOPIA on Jeju-do, I would like to explain the answer to the age-old question: Again, "What came first, the chicken or the egg?"

B. The Egg

On January 9 through 19 in 1991, I conducted an eleven-day seminar, 18 hours-a-day, in Moscow, with 87 Japanese Karate students. Of those 87 students, five of them dropped out but 82 went on to graduate as Jhoon Rhee Black Belts even though, prior to my seminar, most had taken Japanese Karate, some of them for decades. On the eleventh day, I conducted a 15-hour Q & A session. I was able to answer every question for all 15 hours. The last question from the audience was the ancient paradox: "Which came first: the chicken or the egg?" As I have explained before, I gave four reasons why the egg has to come first.

Reason 1: There is no living creature born that grows smaller in size after birth. Try to find any such living creature. Which is smaller – the chicken or the egg?

Reason 2: Every thing we create goes from a simpler to a more complicated state. For example, in order to make a car, nuts, bolts, wires, wheels, seats, engine, body, etc. must be made first before assembling them in proper order to create a car. Which is simpler – the chicken or the egg?

Reason 3: When we create a new thing, first we make only one. Writers create only one original manuscript as a model to publish in great quantities; all product-makers create only one model to make a mold for mass production. Surely, the Creator created one male and copied him. Then it was only necessary to change the gender to make the first female. Isn't it more economical to copy, rather than reinvent the same thing again? Which is more economical to copy – the chicken or the egg?

Reason 4: When we create something new, we do so with the intent of making it something with a higher value. Let us go into a grocery store and compare the chicken and the egg. If the egg becomes a chicken, it is creating a higher value. However, if the chicken becomes the egg, it is lowering the value. Which has less value – the chicken or the egg?

Later, I found out the man who asked the question was a philosophy professor at Moscow University. Based on the above four reasons, now we all know the answer to the eternal question. Obviously, the answer must be, the egg. Likewise, it makes more sense to produce one model student before two, four, eight, sixteen model students, and so on. Then, we will be able to produce one model student, classroom, and school, then two, four, eight, sixteen schools, and so on. From the scale of the school, we can move to the scales of villages, then cities, then provinces, then nations, and eventually the world!

I have been proposing the ideas of TRUTOPIA to Jeju-do through a number of radio, television, and newspaper interviews ever since 2001. I knew people thought I was out of my mind. Pursuing the idea tirelessly for the last nine years, I sense the people of Jeju-do are slowly but surely opening their minds to the idea. As I have been stressing how to educate children starting in kindergarten and elementary school, I was invited to give a speech at the Hamduk Elementary School on July 11, 2008.

During the speech, one of my questions to the audience was: "Are drinking and smoking good for children?" Everybody replied: "No, Sir." I asked again: "Does it mean they are good for parents and teachers?" Again, everybody replied even louder: "No, Sir!" Recently, I was told that the principal of the school, Mr. Kim, Jung Don quit smoking after 40 years. I believe it is a good start because the change must take place from the top down.

Chapter VII: Building TRUTOPIA

A. "Lamp of the East"

In 1929, the Nobel-Prize Indian poet Rabindranath Tagore wrote a poem, his famous prophecy that Korea will be the "Lamp of the East" someday. When I first came to America in 1956, I was 25. I had never read the poem, except for its title, until my brother Sam Rhee, the owner of the New York Golf store, sent me a 1997 calendar with the poem printed on it. It inspired me to find in this poem all the key words that I have been stressing in my speeches during the last 45 years.

This was a clear confirmation for me the universal values of TBL will spread throughout the world. I also sensed that Taekwondo must be the forerunner of the prophecy. The poem reads as follows:

> **"Lamp of the East"**
>
> **In the golden age of Asia**
> **Korea was one of the lamp-bearers**
> **And that lamp is waiting to be lighted once again**
> **For the illumination in the East**
>
> **Where the mind is without fear**
> **And the head is held high where knowledge is free**
> **Where the world has not been broken up into**
> **Fragments by narrow domestic walls**
>
> **Where words come out from the depth of truth**
> **Where tireless striving stretches its arms towards perfection**
> **Where the clear stream of reason has not lost its way**
> **Into the dreary desert sand of dead habit**
>
> **Where the mind is led forward by thee into**
> **Ever widening thought and action**
> **Into that heaven of freedom, our father land,**
> **Korea, let our country awake.**
> *Rabindranath Tagore*

I was born to be happy, and I am committed to sharing this happiness with the world through TRUTOPIA, utilizing Taekwondo—an art originating from Korea—and martial arts action philosophy as my medium for communicating this vision. I was born in Korea but became awakened to my vision while living in America and learning from its freedom system of democracy. Also, I feel fortunate and proud that the jurisdiction that became available for me to implement TRUTOPIA happens to be within the borders of South Korea, namely the island province of Jeju-do.

B. Come Join Us in Building TRUTOPIA

By paraphrasing the inspirational words from the great Dr. Martin Luther King, Jr., I would like to summarize my vision of TRUTOPIA:

> **"I have a dream that one day everyone will live in a TRUTOPIA, where everyone is Truthful in order to become Beautiful so that we live in a world of Love—a happy global society."** *Jhoon Rhee*

If I told you 100 years ago that I flew from the US to Korea, you would have thought that I was crazy. If I told you I walked on the moon 50 years ago, you would have thought I was crazy. And if I told you that soon I'd send a written document within a minute from Seoul to Washington, DC, just 40 years ago, you would have thought I was crazy. Today, they are all reality. Today I am crazy to say TRUTOPIA will be a reality within the 21st century, but I will be a visionary to the people of 22nd century, if I succeed.

Now, I have a vision and a plan of action to rebuild our world "where everyone is happy with every breath of life." All visions throughout history were considered crazy at the beginning, and then they came true. Everybody is born to be healthy, wealthy, and happy with this enlightened wisdom obtained through living an absolutely honest life with compassion for people.

Our world will be perfect only when people are humanly perfect. How can we produce humanly perfect people? Since people are products of education, this world needs new teaching ideas that can motivate people to take positive actions to make a better world beginning from within.

In order to achieve 100 years of wisdom in a body 21 years young, we must live a stress-free life through a positive lifestyle. The only way to live a stress-free life is to never make a mistake knowingly. If we do not try to realize this vision today, our world will remain as it has been, in the status-quo where human suffering continues throughout history.

I would like to remind you by sharing the Three Golden Rules for creating saints out of your three and four-year-olds:

1. **Lead by example.**
2. **Never fail to correct their mistakes with a smile until good habits are formed.**
3. **Lead by example continually.**

Let us commit ourselves to be humanly perfect, to build TRUTOPIA together by creating one humanly perfect and happy person at a time. Let each of us rebuild the world by becoming a true example to our children, students, and fellow human beings by living in TBL. Let us cultivate and maintain health in our bodies and minds by practicing Strength, Honesty, and Knowledge. If we develop these three basic human qualities while never making a mistake knowingly, we will achieve human perfection. If we take this transformation a step further and properly guide our future generations, this way will become the status-quo, and thereby make it natural to build TRUTOPIA. People in society have been conditioned in certain ways for thousands of years leading to the lifestyle we live today. It is time to try something new. We have all the tools and materials needed to build TRUTOPIA.

Appendix

A. Author's Biography

Grand Master Jhoon Rhee, widely recognized for introducing and popularizing Taekwondo in the United States, Europe, and the former USSR, came to America from Korea in 1956. Today, Taekwondo schools bearing his name are scattered across the country and around the world. In 1980, he retired from instructing at his schools in order to devote his time to working out, expanding his schools, and traveling the world to deliver motivational speeches on the Taekwondo philosophy, TRUTOPIA.

Grand Master Rhee befriended and trained together with fellow martial arts pioneer Bruce Lee. He also taught World Heavyweight Champion Muhammad Ali the "Accu-Punch," which Ali used to knock out Richard Dunn, the British Champion, in the first two-minutes and five-seconds of the fifth round of his title defense in Munich, Germany in 1976.

Later, Grand Master Rhee was the coach for Muhammad Ali in his fight in Tokyo, Japan on June 26, 1976 against Antonio Inoki, the Japanese wrestling champion, which ended in a draw. Grand Master Rhee accompanied Muhammad Ali to Korea the very next day. There were over a million fans of Ali who showed up to welcome him in the streets from Kimpo Airport to Seoul. Ali and Grand Master Rhee received a spectacular open-car parade.

Grand Master Rhee's martial arts program and philosophy of discipline, respect, and personal responsibility were developed into a curriculum which was adopted by eight District of Columbia elementary schools in the early 1990s.

Among Grand Master Rhee's well-known celebrity Black Belt students are Tony Robbins, Jack Valenti, and over a dozen members in the US Congress. Grand Master Jhoon Rhee is a legend on Capitol Hill, where he has trained more than 350 members of Congress in Taekwondo, three mornings a week from 7:00-8:00 a.m. since June 5, 1965. His goal is to teach members of Congress until June 5, 2015 to make it 50 years of volunteer service to personally thank America for what it did for South Korea during the Korean War as well as many other contributions to the world.

Among Grand Master Rhee's Black Belt students from the US Congress, are Bob Borski (D-PA), Bill Chappell (D-FL), Mike Espy (D-MS), Richard Ichord (D-MO), Jesse Jackson, Jr. (D-IL), James M. Jeffords (I-VT), Mel Levine (D-CA), Bob Livingston (R-LA), Carolyn Maloney (D-NY), Mike McIntyre (D-NC), Toby Roth (R-WI), Bob Schaffer (R-CO), Gerry Sikorski (D-MN), Nick Smith (R-MN), Ted Stevens (R-AK), Richard Swett (D-NH), James Symington (D-MO), Gene Taylor, (D-MS), and Milton Young (R-ND).

Grand Master Rhee's other famous students include Xavier Becerra (D-CA), Joe Biden (D-DE), Walter Fauntroy (D-DC), Quinton Burdick (D-ND), John Boehner (R-OH), Howard Cannon (D-NV), Ben Chandler (D-KY), Peter DeFazio (D-OR), Eni Faleomavaega (D-AS), Tom Foley (D-WA), Newt Gingrich (R-GA), Bill Gradison, Jr. (R-OH), Peter Hoekstra (R-MI), Duncan Hunter (R-CA), Jack Kingston (R-GA), Dan Lungren (R-CA), Mike McIntyre (D-NC), Gregory Meeks (D-NY), Barbara Mikulski (D-MD), Joseph Montoya (D-MT), Jim Moran (D-VA), Connie Morella (R-MD), Jim Nussle (R-IA), Earl Pomeroy (D-KY), Ileana Ros-Lehtinen (R-FL), Richard Schweiker (R-PA), E. Clay Shaw, Jr. (R-FL), Christopher Shays (R-CT), Ike Skelton (D-MO), Floyd Spence (R-SK), Charles Taylor (R-NC), and Don Young (R-AK).

Grand Master Rhee has been truly impressed by America for over the past half-century, not only in his brain but also in his heart. Grand Master Rhee has envisioned that a happy global society is ahead of us before the end of 21st Century.

He lived a difficult life in Korea, especially after the Korean War, when most Koreans faced widespread poverty and struggled for basic necessities following the civil war. When he first arrived in America (San Francisco Airport), Grand Master Rhee said to himself, "What a contrast! I was in a hell yesterday and now I am in a paradise the next day." He wanted to find out what was the root of America's strength. He discovered it was the noblest political mission statement ever created by any country. He was inspired by the goal of American Manifest Destiny with the United States holding "the responsibility of serving as the vanguard nation for the moral and political emancipation of not just America but also for all humankind."

> **"Liberty is the gift of God not the government. The purpose of government is to protect that liberty not to destroy it."** *George Mason*

This goal inspired Grand Master Rhee to begin a new way of life. For the last 45 years, he has been trying to think, talk, and live with truth, to make TBL his new living habits and way of life. Utopia, known as wishful thinking, could be an actual destiny for the world. To show this realistic goal, Grand Master Rhee coined a new word, TRUTOPIA, to express his firm belief that this is not simply fantasy but a potential reality.

B. Contact Information

To Contact Grand Master Jhoon Rhee
Fax: 703-532-1667
jhoonrhee@gmail.com
http://www.JhoonRhee.com

C. Recommended Readings

The Making of George Washington by General William Wilbur
Published by Coxton Printers, First Edition February 1970

5000 Year Leap by E. Cleon Skousen
Published by the National Center for Constitutional Studies, First Edition in 1981

Bruce Lee and I by Jhoon Rhee
Published by MVM Books, First Edition in 2000

Dr. Kun Jae Rhee (1881 – 1973) is my grandfather who loved and influenced my life more than anyone else. Among his ten surviving grandsons, four of them are publicly recognized. Dr. Sue goo Rhee is known as the top scientist in Korea today; my brother Jungoo Rhee (Sam), is a poet and President of the Seoul University Alumnae Association in America; Jung-goo (my cousin) served as Korean Marine ports Administrator; I am known as the father of Taekwondo in the Western Hemisphere.

My grandfather received his Doctorate Diploma from the Sung Kyun Kwan University in Confucius philosophy, on January 3, 1900. He lost his chance to become a governor of Kyungsang Bukdo due to the Japanese occupation of Korea in 1910.

Mrs. Rhee, Kayim Hong, my mother (1906 – 1994), raised five children who are still all living healthy lives as of 2010. Their ages range from 70 to 86.

My father, Chairman Jin Hoon Rhee (1909 – 1965), served as the Chairman of Suwon City, Korea from 1961 to 1962. He has two sons and three daughters, who all lead successful lives. His three daughters are Namgoo 86, Ahngoo 83, and Ongoo 74, and his sons are Jhoongoo 80, Jungoo (Sam) 70.

From 1958 to 1960, when I was a freshman at Southwest Texas State Teacher's College in San Marcos, Texas, I used a motor scooter to move around the campus.

Prayer

Adapted from Robert Louis Stevenson and distributed at the Golden Wedding Anniversary of Robert Lee Bunting and Byrd Sorsby Bunting, San Marcos, Texas, August 6, 1961.

Lord, behold our family and friends here assembled. We thank Thee for the places in which we dwell and for the government under which we dwell; for the love that unites us; for the peace accorded us this day; for the hope with which we expect the morrow; for the health, the work, the food and the bright skies that make our lives so delightful; for our friends in all parts of the earth; and for our friendly helpers on this occasion.

Let peace abound in the lives of our small company and throughout thy universe. Purge out of every heart the lurking grudge. Give us grace and strength to forbear and to persevere. Offenders, give us the grace to 'cept and to forgive offenders. Forgetful ourselves, help us to bear heerfully the forgetfulness of others.

Give us courage and gaiety and the quiet mind. Spare to us our friends, soften to us our enemies. Bless us, if it may be, in all our innocent endeavors. If it may not be, give us the strength to encounter that which is to come, that we may be brave in peril, constant in tribulation, temperate in wrath and in all changes of fortune, and down to the gates of death loyal and loving one to another and to Thee.

As the clay to the potter, as the windmill to the wind, as children of their sire, we beseech of Thee this help and mercy for Christ's sake.

Mr. and Mrs. Robert L. Bunting were my sponsors to study in the USA in 1957. Without Mr. & Mrs. Bunting's sponsorship, I wouldn't be living in America and Taekwondo may not have been introduced to the world in such a positive and successful way.

My Mother Kayim Hong Rhee sitting in the center with four children. From the left are Sam, Ongoo, Mother, Jhoongoo and Namgoo.

My Mother Kayim Hong Rhee's 80th birthday party in 1986 at a Buddhist Temple in Maryland.

My Mother Kayim Hong Rhee was proud of her two sons; me on the left and my brother Sam on the right. She was known as "Jhoon's Mother" among the people in the Korean community of the Washington Metropolitan Areas.

My late first wife Hansoon (1934-1995) passed away after 29 happy years of marriage. Front row from the left are Hansoon, me, and Meme. Back row from left are Bryan Oh, Joanne Oh, Chun, Linda Rhee and Jimmy. This photo was taken in 1990.

Theresa and I on our wedding day. From the left are the four best men; son Chun, son Jimmy, Rep. Toby Roth, and my brother Sam Rhee; Theresa and I are in the center; the four bridesmaids are Theresa's sisters Jungdae, Sookja, my daughter Meme, and Sheryl Etelson (a member of my staff).

To celebrate my one year wedding anniversary with Theresa on July 21, 1998, we took a cruise to the Bahamas. Pictured are me, my wife Theresa, and my mother-in-law Jungwon Suh.

Here I am in my office with a future Saint. Masters Tim and Shannon Wong promised to raise their first son Conner to be a Saint by the time he turns 21.

Masters Barry Shakelford and Francis Pineda demonstrate flying side kicks at their Jhoon Rhee Institute in Arlington, VA studio. This two man team in Arlington, VA run the most profitable Jhoon Rhee Studio and have a waiting list of students hoping to join every month.

Two of my students stand on chairs as I am breaking two boards that are held at a height of seven and one half feet above the ground. The students had to stand on chairs to hold the boards that high.

I am with world renowned Basketball Champion Wilt Chamberlain at the US Bicentennial Sports Awards in the Shoreham Hotel. Wilt Chamberlain was awarded the "Basketball Man of the Century". I was awarded the "Martial Arts Man of the Century," and Muhammad Ali was awarded "Boxer of the Century" in 1976.

Mrs. Etty Allen, the Washington Redskins Coach George Allen, and I are enjoying one of my Taekwondo students demonstrations being performed in 1974.

I am receiving the Bicentennial Sports Award as the "Martial Arts Man of the Century" from the world renowned Columnist Jack Anderson in 1976.

Posing for a picture with my friend, the World Light Weight Boxing Champion Sugar Ray Leonard.

Muhammad Ali is answering questions from the Japanese Press at his arrival in Tokyo. Ali fought the Japanese wrestler Antonio Inoki June 26, 1976. I am standing next to Ali while he is being interviewed.

Boxing Champion Muhammad Ali and I are chatting after the Boxer Muhammad Ali verses Wrestler Antonio Inoki fight in Tokyo, Japan on June 26, 1976. I served as Ali's Martial Arts Coach.

I invited World Boxing Champion Muhammad Ali to Seoul, Korea on June 27, 1976 after the famous Ali vs. Inoki fight in Tokyo, Japan on June 26, 1976. We just landed at the Kimpo International Airport in Korea.

I am with President Leonid Kravchuk of Ukraine (from 1991-1995) on Capitol Hill. I visited President Kravchuk in Ukraine in 1992, two months prior to this meeting.

Senator Milton Young of North Dakota is breaking two one-inch boards held by me on September 19, 1977. This action was shown in the TV campaign proving that he is still young and energetic at age 81. He defeated William Guy by 200 votes in the 1977 Senate Race of North Dakota. I was praised for the suggestion.

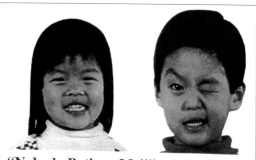

"Nobody Bothers Me!!"
"Nobody Bothers Me Either!!"

The "Nobody Bothers Me" TV commercial which aired in the 1970s and 1980s, starred my daughter Meme 3, and my son Chun age 4 in 1972. At the publication of this book in 2010, Meme is a successful Psychotherapist in Beverly Hills, CA and Chun is a Taekwondo Master and runs the Jhoon Rhee Falls Church, VA school.

My students Kehilian, Francis Pineda, Arnold Schwarzenegger who was Chairman of the President's Council on Physical Fitness and Sports, Carmichael, Simon and me in 1984.

My brother Sam Rhee and I visiting former Ambassador and publisher Boris Pyadyshev of the International Affairs Magazine, the official Journal of the USSR Ministry of Foreign Affairs in 1991.

I was invited to a Congressional Conference in September 2010 on Capitol Hill, where Mr. Bob Schieffer was the speaker of the event.

Mr. Kim, Duk Soo, one of the most famous Korean Farm Dance drummers posing with me.

Here I am squaring off with famous Japanese Sumo Champion Konishiki.

Former Japanese professional wrestler and a member of the Japanese National Assembly, Antonio Inoki and I presented our speeches at the Yong-in University of Korea for some of the university's students.

Speaker Tom Foley breaking two one-inch-thick boards with his elbow strike at the 1993 Jhoon Rhee Championships in the Shoreham Hotel in Washington, DC on August 1, 1993.

The famous Russian Sculptor Gregory Pototsky and his beautiful wife Olga presenting my head sculpture at the United Nations, where I delivered a speech titled Lead by Example Action Philosophy on April 10, 2007.

Chuck Norris holding boards for my board breaking demonstration in Dallas, Texas at the Annual Texas Martial Arts Conference after my speech Born to be Healthy, Wealthy, and Happy.

A luncheon meeting was held in the Rayburn House Office Building to discuss a possible US Congressional Taekwondo Diplomacy visit to North Korea and further to discuss the possibility of a Taekwondo town in the middle of the Demilitarized Zone in 1997. From the left are Jack Anderson, Rep. Nick Smith, Speaker Tom Foley, John Marriot of Marriot Hotels, me, Curtis Lee, Rep Bob Schaffer and three N. Korean delegates headed by Lee, Chong Hyuk.

US Congressman Toby Roth and I were awarded honorary Doctor's degrees from Kyung Nam University on April 11, 1995. From the left are US Congressman Toby Roth, President Park, Jae Kyu of Kyung Nam University, and me.

My wife Theresa and I were invited by former Speaker and later US Ambassador of Japan, Tom Foley, to his residence in Tokyo, Japan for a luncheon with he and his wife, Mrs. Martha Foley in 1995.

My daughter Meme Rhee with First Lady Hillary Clinton and I at the 1995 State Dinner in the White House.

Talking with President Bill Clinton at the 1995 White house State Dinner after the Korean War Memorial Dedication Ceremony.

Former Governor of Virginia, George Allen and I embrace while Mrs. Susan Allen looks on with a big smile.

I am visiting Speaker Dennis Hastert for a meeting with former Korean political party leader of the Hannaradang, Lee, Hae Chang in 1999.

Former Korean Congressman Young Kwang Kim, Former US Secretary of Agriculture Mike Espy, Former US Congressman Bob Livingston, and I visiting with Former Prime Minister of Korea J. P. Kim of Korea in July 1999.

I am with the Honorable Connie Morella of Maryland who was a member of the US Congressional Taekwondo Club in 2000.

I am standing at the podium in the White House Press Room.

My wife Theresa and I are with Speaker Newt Gingrich on Capitol Hill in 1997.

Jhoon Rhee Students' Reunion Dinner Party celebrating Jhoon Rhee Day declared by the Mayor of Washington, DC Anthony Williams on June 28, 2003. The first Jhoon Rhee Taekwondo School was opened on June 28, 1962, 41 years earlier. This photo shows students who joined me prior to 1980.

Jhoon Rhee Students' Reunion Dinner Party celebrating Jhoon Rhee Day declared by the Mayor of Washington, DC Anthony Williams on June 28, 2003. The first Jhoon Rhee Taekwondo School was opened on June 28, 1962, 41 years earlier. This photo shows students who joined me after 1980.

The honorable Lee, Soo Sung, former Prime Minister of Korea, my daughter Meme Rhee, me, Grand Master Um, Unkyu, and Jungkil Kim, former President of the Korea Taekwondo Association, posing at the 10021 Club International Kick-Off Conference on March 4, 2002 in the Marriot Hotel in Seoul, Korea.

US Rep. Ileana Ros-Lehtinen with me after one of her Taekwondo classes in 1990.

I am chatting with Rev. Kim, Changhwan and a former member of the National Assembly of Korea, Honorable Kim, Young Kwang.

I am with my friend and respected actress, the late Yau, Woongey.

Jhoon Rhee's One on One Team: PD Kim, Taeuhk, Ms. Lee, Hyangsoo, Mr. Lim, Iksang, the Honorable Pete Sessions, me, and Mr. Lee, Ingab posing after the Jhoon Rhee's One on One TV Talk Show. The show is shown in 189 countries by the Arirang Televsion Network System.

Master of Ceremonies Dong Guen Kim volunteered to support the 10021 Club in Seoul, Korea on March 4, 2002.

Standing with Mike Espy, former Secretary of Agriculture.

Master Alexander Korobov, Deputy Secretary of Education Boris Zhebrovski, and me after my speech on Born to be Healthy, Wealthy, and Happy.

Here I am with US Secretary of Labor Elaine Chao and my wife Theresa Rhee before my speech for the Labor Department staff members on Born to be Healthy, Wealthy, and Happy in October 2003.

Sashar and Mishar Muradbekovich, Jhoon Rhee Taekwondo Masters, demonstrate their awesome kicking power at the Jhoon Rhee Internationals.

My daughter Meme, CNN's Larry King, and me posing for a photo after the Larry King Talk Show in 1991.

UNSG Ban, Ki-Moon, Theresa Rhee, me, and my brother Sam Rhee after my speech at the United Nations on April 10, 2007. The subject of the speech was Mending Our Troubled World through Lead by Example Action Philosophy.

White House Luncheon honoring ten Russian Educational Delegates headed by the Superintendent of Moscow Public Schools Ernest Bakirov, who were all my guests.

Assistant Secretary of the US State Department Robert Gallucci, Korean Ambassador Lee, Tae Shik, and me in the Watergate Hotel.

My good friends Mr. Shin, Sangok, the most famous movie director in Korea and his beautiful wife, Choi, Eunhee, who was the number one actress for several decades in Korea.

I was the guest of Mr. Boris Notkin's Goodnight Moscow TV Show on September 13, 1990 in Moscow, USSR.

Pat Boone is a singer, actor, TV Host, producer, songwriter, author, motivational speaker, family man, humanitarian, and a man unafraid to air his view. I met Pat Boone at one of his patriotic speeches to the US Congress.

I was invited to Masters Allen Steen's 60th Birthday Party in Dallas Texas. Masters Steen and Burleson are the two original leaders of the Jhoon Rhee Taekwondo organization.

Congressman Bob Livingston breaking two one-inch boards with his powerful sidekick while Mike Coles and I hold the boards.

US Congressional Taekwondo Club members with Speaker Tom Foley and Jhoon Rhee's World and National Champions at the 1993 National Championships, August 1, 1993, Shoreham Hotel, Washington, DC.

When the six US Congressional Delegates headed by Hon. John Myers and John Dingell visited Seoul, Vice Speaker of Korea, Hon. Oh, Seung and I hosted a dinner reception with Korean VIPs in the Samchungak Restaurant of Seoul in 1998.

Here I am being presented with a plaque honoring my 45 years of volunteer service of teaching Taekwondo to members of the United States Congress. Meme Rhee, Chun Rhee, Bob Livingston, Dick Swett, Trent Franks, James Symington, Connie Morella, Toby Roth, Katherine Harris, Linda Rhee and Jimmy Rhee. The two gentlemen sitting on the floor are Kirk Pelt and Y. K. Kim.

Hyungwon Kang and me at my 80th birthday celebration.

Friends, family, students and former students are gathered in the House Cannon Office Building Caucus Room on Capital Hill, Washington, DC on September 30, 2010 to celebrate my 45 years of volunteer service of teaching Taekwondo to members of Congress and my 80th birthday. Photo Courtesy: Hyungwon Kang/Senior Staff Photographer/Editor/Reuters

Photo Index